MICRO-FINANCE FOR AGRICULTURE DEVELOPMENT

MICRO-FINANCE
FOR
AGRICULTURE DEVELOPMENT

Edited by
Dr. R.N. Misra
Centre for Management Studies, SMIT
Ankushpur, Berhampur
Orissa
&
G. Chandrayya
Lecturer
Deptt. of Commerce
Government College (Autonomous)
Rajmundry

D P H

DISCOVERY PUBLISHING HOUSE PVT. LTD.
NEW DELHI-110 002

First Published-2010

ISBN 978-81-8356-649-0

Published by:

DISCOVERY PUBLISHING HOUSE PVT. LTD.
4831/24, Ansari Road, Prahlad Street
Darya Ganj, New Delhi-110002 (India)
Phone: 23279245, 43764432 • Fax: 91-11-23253475
E-mail: parul.wasan@gmail.com
info@discoverypublishinggroup.com
Website: www.discoverypublishinggroup.com

Printed at:

Dynamic Printers,

Preface

Basically, the economy of our country is rural in character. In India land represents the chief wealth of the Nation. Till today agriculture consider as important industry which need due consideration. Out of the various factors, for the growth & development of agriculture, timely and adequate finance by the Financing Institutions is highly essential. Supply of credit and its proper use will increase the production and productivity of the agricultural sector. If loan is not used in a proper way it will not generate the repaying capacity of the borrowers and it restrict the repayment of loan and create a burden for institutional agencies and government.

On the basis of the project report submitted by Mr. G. Chandrayya, Department of commerce, Govt. College (Auto), Rajmundry on the basis of the recommendation of Principal, UGC authority has kind enough to provide some financial assistance for conducting two days National Seminar at Govt. College (Auto) Rajmundry, on the topic "Finance to the Agriculture by the Institutional Agencies and Recoveries". The college conducted the seminar on 17 and 18 July 2009 at Rajmundry, Andhra Pradesh.

Timely recovery of loan from the borrowers is a serious concern. Nearly 50% of the loans are due at borrowers' level. Unless the loan is not repaid in time it become over dues and it will create a number of problems for banking, government and other sectors. And it will curtail the economic growth of the country.

Editors

ACKNOWLEDGEMENT

We are very much thankful to all paper contributors for their kind help and cooperation for providing their article in time.

We express our special thanks to Mr. Tilak Wasan, Director of the Discovery Publishing House Pvt. Ltd., New Delhi for his kind consent to publish the book in time, in spite of his busy schedule. His attitude is to help us to write this book, so we are very much thankful to him on behalf of the all paper writers. We are also thankful to the son of Tilak Wasan who is now taking all care relating to publishing affairs of Discovery Publishing House Pvt. Ltd.

We are also thankful to all staff members of Discovery Publishing House Pvt. Ltd., New Delhi, for their kind help and co-ordination for publishing the book in time. We are also very much thankful to the UGC authority for sanctioning financial assistance for conducting two days National Seminar at Government College (Autonomous) Rajamundry, Andhra Pradesh.

R.N. Misra
G. Chandrayya

Contents

Contents

1

Financing Style of Institutional Agencies Towards Agricultural Sector – A Study

Dr. Rabi N. Misra[1]
Mr. Rookesh Misra[2]

Basically the economy of India is rural in character. In India land represents the chief wealth of the national. Indian agriculture is still in the primitive form and the agricultural potential of the country is yet to be exploited. From among the various factors, non-availability of adequate and timely agricultural credit is one of the reasons for low productivity. Agriculture is an important industry which warrants due consideration. Credit is highly essential in the context of new strategies in agricultural field consequent upon the introduction of high yielding varieties.

Source of credit is an important factor which influences the propensity to borrow. Credit supply and its proper use are two main important instrument for agricultural growth. Use of credit for productive and unproductive purposes depends upon the behavioral attitude/supply of credit to the borrowers. If borrowing is utilized for productive purposes it may generate its own means of repayment. But diversion of credit creates some major problems and ultimately restricts the repayment.

[1] Professor, PGCMS, B.P.U.T., S.M.I.T., Ankushpur, Berhampur.
[2] HR Manager and Research Scholar.

About Sample District

The sample district of Ganjam in the state of Orissa was formed on 1st April, 1936. The meaning of the word "Ganjam" means "Ganja-I-am" which means "Granary of the world". The district is surrounded by Boudh-Kandhamal district of Orissa in north, Srikakulam district of Andhra Pradesh and Gajapati district of Orissa in south. Bay of Bengal and Puri district in the east. The total area of the district is 8,206 square kilometres having three sub-divisions, 22 blocks, 3212 villages, 19 towns, 14 thasils and 12 assembly constituencies. The climate of the Ganjam district is charaterised by homogeneous temperature throughout the year. Humidity is very high. The maximum and minimum temperature recorded during the past five year was 31.5° and 23.7° Celsius respectively. The average rainfall of the district is 129.56 cm per annum and rain occurs between second week of June to early October.

Relevance of the Study

Orissa occupies an important place in the agricultural map of India. Agriculture is considered the primary industry in Orissa. In the sample district Ganjam a considerable number of population (nearly 60%) are engaged in the agricultural sector. But agricultural productivity and standard of living of agriculturists' of the sample district is very poor. Timely and proper finance are very important factors for high agricultural productivity. Regarding finance to agriculturists of sample district three banks like Commercial Banks, Regional Rural Banks and Co-operative Banks are taken for the purpose of the study. Besides institutional financing, non-institutional agencies are also playing a vital role in lending to the agriculturists of the study region.

Methodology Applied

The data for the study are collected from two sources, that is from primary sources and secondary sources. For sampling design keeping in view the relevance and scope of the study it was decided to choose borrowers on the basis of representative sampling instead of taking the whole universe. For this purpose

300 primary data are to be collected through administration of suitable questionnaire prepared for the purpose by considering the pros and cons of the study by meeting borrowers personally. The study has covered a period of eight years from 2000-2001 to 2007-2008. Data for secondary nature will collected for the secondary source that is from books, journals, periodicals and others.

Limitation of the Study

Due to limitation of time and resources only one district of Orissa has been selected as sample district and only seven years have been taken for the purpose. Three hundred beneficiaries have been selected at random for the sample district. The information supplied by the sample borrowers at the time of survey cannot be taken as hundred per cent accurate. Similarly hundred per cent accuracy cannot be attached to the secondary data used in the study.

Analysis of the Study

The different sources supplying agricultural credit are co-operatives, commercial banks and Regional Rural banks under the fold of institutional sources. The financing style of institutional agencies of the sample district has explained here from the information supplied by the sample borrowers at the time of survey.

Borrowing According to Caste

The borrowers of the sample district are classified into three categories *i.e.* Scheduled Caste, Scheduled Tribe and General. The flow of credit according to caste-wise is illustrated in Table 1.1.

Table 1.1 reveals the general caste borrowers of the sample district have availed 65.6% of the total amount supplied during the period of study. But backward loaness jointly availed 34.4%.

Borrowing According to the Literacy

Literacy also plays a vital role in borrowing of agricultural loan. Borrowing according to the literacy/illiteracy of the sample district is illustrated in Table 1.2.

Table 1.1. Distribution of credit according to caste-wise (2000-01 to 2007-08)

Name of District	*S.T*		*S.C*		*General*		*Total*	
	N.B	*Amount Rs. in Thousand*	*N.B*	*Amount Rs. in Thousand*	*N.B*	*Amount Rs. in Thousand*	*N.B*	*Amount Rs. in Thousand*
Ganjam	84 (28.0%)	114.9 (18.4%)	56 (18.7%)	100.2 (16.0%)	160 (53.3%)	409.9 (65.6%)	300 (100%)	625.0 (100%)

Source: Complied from questionnaire.
N.B = No. of borrowers, S.T. = Scheduled Tribe, S.C. = Scheduled Caste.

Table 1.2. Borrowing according to literacy and illiteracy

Name of District	*Illiterate*		*Literate*		*Total*	
	N.B	*Amount Rs. in Thousand*	*N.B*	*Amount Rs. in Thousand*	*N.B*	*Amount Rs. in Thousand*
Ganjam	106 (35.4%)	192.0 (30.7%)	194.0 (64.6%)	433.0 (69.3%)	300 (100%)	625.0 (100%)

Source: Compiled from questionnaire.
N.B = No. of borrowers.

From the Table 1.2 it is clear that 64.6% of literate sample borrowers can able to get loan of 69.3%, where as illiterate borrowers are able to get 30.7% of loan amount sanctioned for the purpose.

Pre-Borrowing Expenses

The sample borrowers generally take the help of middlemen, village touts, NGO personnel and others to obtain institutional credit. The borrowers has to pay some amount for their services like transport charges pocket expenses etc. the borrowers generally meet such expenses from the non-institutional agencies and borrowers meet such expenses after getting the loan from institutional agencies. The detail is explained in Table 1.3.

Table 1.3 reveals that out of the total supply of loan Rs. 41.7 thousand or 6.8% have been spent for pre borrowing expenses by sample loanees.

Table 1.3. Pre-borrowing Expenses met by sample borrowers

Name of District	*Number of Borrowers*	*Pre-borrowing Expenses Rs. in Thousand*	*Balance with borrows for use Rs. in Thousand*	*Total Credit Suplly Rs. in Thousand*
Ganjam	300	41.8 (6.8%)	583.2 (93.2%)	625.0 (100%)

Source: Complied from questionnaire.

Sufficient to Meet the Purpose

The loans provided by the sample borrowers are not satisfied due to insufficient of loan amount. This is explained in the Table 1.4.

Table 1.4. Sufficiency of institutional loan to meet the purpose of the sample borrowers

Name of District	*Number of Borrowers*	*Sufficient to meet the purpose*	*Not sufficient to meet the purpose*
Ganjam	300	24.0 (8.0%)	276.0 ((92.0%)

Source: Complied from questionnaire.

According to Table 1.4, 276 or 92% of the borrowers are not satisfied with the institutional finance.

Finance as Per Age Group

The sample beneficiaries of the study district have been devided into five categories in accordance with their age group. The finance provided by the banks according to the age group is explained in Table 1.5.

From Table 1.5 it reveals that the borrowers belong to age group of 40-50 can able to arrange a lion share of loan from institutional agencies.

Term–wise Finance

The financing institutions advance three types of loans; short term loans to meet short term needs; medium term loans meant for semi urgent requirement like purchase of agricultural implements and long term loans for capital expenditure of the agriculturists. The term-wise is explained in Table 1.6.

Table 1.5. Loan provided to the sample borrowers according to their age group

Name of District	*Age Group*	*Number of Borrowers*	*Amount Rs. in Thousand*
Ganjam	20-30	29	23.3
	30-40	77	168.5
	40-50	117	383.0
	50-60	68	47.5
	60-above	09	2.7
	Total	300	625.0

Source: Compiled from questionnaire.

Table 1.6 reveals that in case of long term loan 19% of borrowers are able to get 62% of loan.

Table 1.6. Term-wise Finance

Name of District	*Terms*	*Number of Borrowers*	*Amount Rs. in Thousand*
Ganjam	Short-Term Loan	171	208.7
	Medium-Term Loan	72	176.3
	Long-Term Loan	57 (19%)	385.0 (62%)
	Total	300	625.0

Source: Compiled from questionnaire.

Finance According to Mode

The financial institutions generally provided credit to the borrowers in cash, kind or both cash and kind. This is illustrated in Table 1.7.

From Table 1.7 it reveals that the banking authority provide more fund to the borrowers on cash and kind component 55%).

Table 1.7. Mode-wise Finance

Name of District	*Cash*		*Kind*		*Cash & Kind*		*Total*	
	N.B	*Amount Rs. in Thousand*	*N.B*	*Amount Rs. in Thousand*	*N.B*	*Amount Rs. in Thousand*	*N.B*	*Amount Rs. in Thousand*
Ganjam	91	102.0	64	174.5	145	348.5 (55%)	300	625.0

Source: Compiled from questionnaire.
N.B = No of borrowers, T.B = Total borrowers

Suggestions

A few humble suggestions are put forth here under to contain the situation.

1. Banking authority should take very reasonable time to sanction agricultural loan.
2. Credit may not be sanctioned according to the approved scheme of the lending institution, but according to the need of the borrowers.
3. Post-lending supervision and approaching the borrowers personally for proper use of the fund will tempt the loanee to use the fund for productive purpose.
4. The employees of lending institutions should develop a positive attitude in creating friendly relation with borrowers. They have to gain fairly adequate knowledge about behaviour, personal need and character of the borrowers.

REFERENCES

Dadhich, C. L, *Overdues in farm Co-operative Credit,* Popular Prakashan, Bombay.

Economic Survey of Orissa-1907-08, Bureau of Statistics and Economics, Orissa, Bhubaneswar.

Misra, R. N, *India Economy,* Anmol Publication, New Delhi.

Patnaik, U.C, *Introduction to Co-operatgive Managemen,* Kalyani Publishers, New Delhi.

2

Finance Problems of Farmers and Solutions

K. Anurupa Rao,[1]
P. Chandra Shekhar[2]

Introduction

Agriculture refers to the production of food and goods through farming and forestry. Agriculture was the key development that led to the rise of civilization; with the husbandry of domesticated animals and plants (*i.e.,* crops) creating food surpluses that enabled the development of more densely populated and stratified societies. The study of agriculture is known as agricultural science.

Agriculture encompasses a wide variety of specialties and techniques, including ways to expand the lands suitable for plant rising, by digging water-channels and other forms of irrigation. Cultivation of crops on arable land and the pastoral herding of livestock on rangeland remain at the foundation of agriculture. In the past century there has been increasing concern to identify and quantify various forms of agriculture. In the developed world the range usually extends between sustainable agriculture. In the developed world the range usually extends between sustainable agriculture (*e.g.* organic agriculture) and intensive farming (*e.g.* industrial agriculture). Agriculture has played a key role in the development of human civilization. Until the

[1] Asst. Professor, Department of Management Studies, Government Collage (A), Rajahmundry. E-mail : anuruparao.mba@gmail.com
[2] Government College (A), Rajahmudry,
E-mail: pchandrashekhar.mba@gmail.com

Industrial Revolution, the vast majority of the human population labored in agriculture. Development of agricultural techniques has steadily increased agricultural productivity, and the widespread diffusion of these techniques during a time period is often called an agricultural revolution. A remarkable shift in agricultural practices has occurred over the past century in response to new technologies.

India basically is an agricultural country which provides livelihood to most of its population. In fact, the farmers in India are regarded as the real hero's for Agriculture is the way of life, a tradition which for centuries has shaped the thought, the outlook, the culture and the economic life of the people of India. Agriculture is the oldest profession of the people of India. Indian agriculture has passed through various phases like self-sufficiency. India has to sustain 16% of the world's population on 2.4% of the global land area. In India, agriculture contributes about 21% of the national GDP and over 100 million families of farmers manage almost 142 million hectares. However, Indian agricultural sector needs special attention to sustain our national economy.

But out of the various factors that determine the development of agriculture in India, Finance is the major factor which needs due consideration. The marginal farmers are not able to increase the agricultural productivity due to lack of funds. Mahatma Gandhi once remarked that India resides in its villages. Most of the Indian population relies directly or indirectly on the agriculture or agro-based industries. The fate of the farmers determines the fate of the nation's economy. The prosperity of the nation is, therefore, directly dependent upon the farmers prosperity.

At present, nearly 40% of the total national income of India is earned by the working population engaged in agriculture. Agricultural sector contributes a lot to the growing needs of the nation for large capital resources. In this regard, agriculture can be viewed as a potent instrument for rapid economic development and rural prosperity.

The significance of financing the agricultural operations in a country like India where hundreds of millions of people obtain their livelihood is very much necessary. This being an important industry needs a large amount of finance. Despite, the fact is that the present agricultural sector is facing severe hurdles in the agricultural credits. This landed the farmers into several financial problems which are ending up with drastic tragedies like farmers suicides.

Objective of the Study

Indian agriculture has been facing a big challenge in the globalization era because production and productivity growth rate has decreased for the past few years. Moreover, it has been slow in absorbing the process of liberalization. The study is one the financial problems of small and marginal farmers.

FINANCIAL PROBLEMS OF FARMERS

The Indian farmers are now-a-days coming across a large number of problems; the major one among them is finance. Due to lack of funds they are not in a position to increase the production to the desired levels. Though the farmers are capable of producing goods crops, they are not able to put their best due to lack of sufficient monetary aid.

Some of the problems faced by the farmers are as under:

High Level of Indebtness

Small and marginal farmers need credit to meet both consumption needs to maintain subsistence levels as well as for production needs to meet the increasing cost of cultivation. Increased costs of indebtness are noted as a major reason for the spurt in the farmers' suicides. Among other reasons for suicides, the prime reason is indebtness. When the crop failed and the prices went down, they had no means to repay the loans. They had no other alternative except ending their lives. The incidence of indebtness among farmers and their families was highest in Andhra Pradesh 82 per cent) followed by Tamilnadu (75 percent) and Punjab (65 per cent).

Role of Credit

The growth in agriculture in the early times was facilitated by the spread of rural credit institutions and improved access to credit. The position of agricultural credit with respect to marginal and small farmers continues to be extremely unsatisfactory. The small and marginal farm holdings account for 42 per cent of agricultural land but the bank credit given to small farmers is very low at just around three per cent.

Size of land holdings (in hectares)

Sources of loans	*>0.4*	*0.41 to 1.00*	*1.01 to 2.00*	*>2.00*
Institutional	42.4	52.8	57.6	66.8
Non-Institutional	57.6	47.2	42.4	33.2

Source: Banking statistical returns, RBI issues IWG-20

The statistical information reveals the truth that small and marginal farmers have less access to institutional sources of about 42 and 53% respectively, whereas the farm holdings of medium and large farmers have better access to institutional sources of finance. Rather the small holding farmers are more attracted towards the non-institutional sources of credit in which 67% of the credit is from non-institutional sources. The percentage of loans from non-institutional sources to large farmers is comparatively less.

Difference in Incomes and Expenditures

This relates to the economic status of the farmers. There is a huge difference in the income and the expenditure levels of the farmers. The pattern of the average income and expenditure levels determine the economic status of the small and marginal farmers as well as of the medium and large farmers. The average expenditure levels increase with the increase in the size of the land holdings.

Difference in income and Expenditure

(in rupees)

Holding size (in ha)	*Income*	*Expenditure*
1 and less than 1	1809	2672
1 to 2	2493	3148
2 to 4	3589	3685
4 to 10	5681	4626
More than 10	9667	6418

The average monthly income and expenditure of the household farmer indicates their economic status. The statistics show that the expenditure levels are higher than the income levels especially for small and marginal farmers. The farmers having holdings of more than 10 hectares have income higher than the expenditure. An analysis of the farm holding levels and the difference in the income and expenditure levels reveals that the small and marginal farmers have low economic status due to huge amounts of debts. These debts force the farmers into deep financial crisis which end up with their suicides..

Dependence on Market

The liberised scenario of price risks has heightened the dependence on market. It has exposed the farmers to fluctuating price regimes. This is of particular concern for small and marginal farmers who do not have the means to cope up with such situations. The entire crop of the small farmers comes to the market at one time. The small cultivators who are heavily indebted have very poor bargaining strength. The Minimum Support Price (MSP) given by the government has not been increased even up to the levels of farmers expenditure. According to the estimated statistics, the income to produce one quintal of paddy ranges from Rs. 1200-Rs. 1500. But the MSP offered by the government is Rs. 900 only. The remaining amount is an additional burden for the farmers for which they need to borrow from other sources and if they are not able to repay the debt for any reasons, it may lead them to take some drastic steps.

Other Factors

In addition to the above stated, the farmers are also facing many other problems like :

(*a*) **Distribution of sub-standard seed to the farmers:** The supply of sub-standard seeds will not result in good crop which again will be a burden to the farmer.

(*b*) **Insurance of crop :** Crop insurance is an uncommon practice with only 4% of the farmers being insured their crop. Compared to 14% of the large farmers, only 2% of sub-marginal farmers, 2% of marginal farmers and 5% of small farmers have crop insurance. In these situations, crop failure due to natural calamities like floods, soil erosion, drought etc. will land the farmers into distress.

(*c*) **Private Participation :** The new economic policies of the government have increased the private participation in the agricultural sector. This has restricted the farmers from acquiring modern agricultural practices like investment in fertilizers, pesticides, electricity and water resources.

SOLUTIONS TO IMPROVE THE AGRICUTURAL SECTOR

1. It is the prime responsibility of the government to take an initiative for decreasing the suicides of farmers. In case of crop failure, the government should lend its hand to the farmers through its policies.
2. Institutional credit and non-institutional credit are the only ways to agriculture. Farmers should be encouraged and awareness should be created especially to small and marginal farmers towards institutional sources. On the other hand, the financial institutions should relax their rules for providing the loans to the farmers.
3. It is the need of the hour for the government to prepare special package for meeting the agrarian crisis and preventing the farmers from taking drastic steps like committing suicides.
4. A stable market price should be given to the crops which can protect the farmers from the price fluctuations. The Minimum Support Price (MSP) should be atleast 50% more than the average cost price.
5. According to the report given by Prof. M.S. Swami Nathan, the government should take initiative to establish a "Farm Income Commission" to suggest ways of ensuring a minimum take home income to farmers.

Conclusion

Indian agriculture has to be modernized by systematic and timely application of modern scientific inputs. Agriculture is not just for economy, it is for society and polity.

REFERENCES

Eenadu

Economic and political weekly

RBI issues

Southern economist

Survey of Indian agriculture 2008

The Hindu

The economic times

3

The Role of Micro-finance for Sustainable Development in India Agricultural Sector

M.V.K. Srinivasa Rao,[1]
T. Hymavathi Kumari[2] *& P. Tirumala*[2]

Introduction

Agricultural production in India depends upon millions of small farmers. It is the intensity of their effort and the efficiency of their technique that will help in raising yields per acre. Because of inadequate financial resources and absence of timely credit facilities at reasonable rates, many of the fanners, even though otherwise willing, are unable to go in for improved seeds and manures or to introduce better methods or techniques. It is, therefore, of the utmost importance that the financial requirements of the farmers are adequately met. Despite a mere 18.5 per cent contribution to the gross domestic product (GDP), agriculture still provides livelihood support to about two-thirds of the country's population. Quite appropriately, agricultural development has been given due importance right from India's First Five-year Plan (1951-56). The country has taken notable strides in the agricultural sector during the last four decades of economic planning where the contours of Indian

1 Associate Professor, PG Courses MBA, Raghu Engineering College, Visakhapatnam. EmailID: mvks_rao@yahoo.co.in
2 Assistant Professors, PG Courses (MBA), Raghu Engineering College, Visakhapatnam Email ID: hymavathi.tenneti@gmail.com & tirupentapati@yahoo.com.

agriculture started showing improvement gradually after the mid-1960s with the introduction of High Yielding Varieties (HYV) of crops. The subsequent emphasis, on the development of agricultural infrastructure for supply of agro-inputs like irrigation, power, water, seed, credit and fertilizers, creation of storage and marketing facilities and provision of adequate and fair distribution of food-grains however could not give an appropriate boost to the growth of agricultural productivity. The main objective of bank nationalization was to direct larger volumes of credit to priority sectors comprising agriculture, small scale industries sector and artisans etc., the share of priority sector was 33.9 per cent in 2000 which has been significantly increased till the present year.

Till Independence in 1947, money lenders and the landlords were the principal sources of rural credit. Over the years, the operations of moneylenders have declined in view of debt relief legislations, the system of licensing money lenders and restrictions on the use and transfer of land as security. Similarly, the abolition of all privileged tenures both in zamindari and Ryotwari areas has discouraged investment by the landlords and larger cultivators. The key problem of those dependent on agriculture, specially the poor, small and marginal farmers and weaker sections of the society, is finance. Therefore, in each Plan period, there has been a continued emphasis on rapid and progressive institutionalization for supply of timely and adequate credit-support to enable those engaged in agriculture to adopt modern agricultural technology and improved agricultural practices for enhanced growth, production and productivity. The traditional concern about accessibility of agricultural credit to the needy rural inhabitants is still alive even after increasing bank branch network, improving Co-operative Banking structure, evolving specialized rural banking institutions (*i.e.,* Regional Rural Banks) and the setting up of various financial agencies like the National Bank for Agriculture and Rural Development (NABARD) in 1982. The impressive quantitative expansion of bank branches and other rural formal financial intermediaries has not really helped in developing an atmosphere of hassle-free qualitative credit flow in the rural economy. We have been focusing on co-operative movements, priority sector lending, operation, supervision and monitoring of rural credit by designated rural financial agencies for the smooth, adequate and timely flow of credit to the rural people. With the disappointing result of these formal agencies, we have now started depending on an innovative model of credit delivery mechanism, popularly known as micro-finance. This micro-finance (MF), after the so-called Grameen Bank revolution in Bangladesh, is the buzz-word these days and is treated as a suitable alternative to formal banking in rural India keeping in view its cost-effectiveness, easy and hassle-free accessibility and in-built process for loan allocation and its recovery.

The objectives of the paper are to: review agricultural credit policies followed in India and assess the trends and progress in credit flow and access; analyze particularly the issues relating to sustainability of the micro-finance programme in Indian agricultural sector and the innovative micro credit schemes adopted by the nationalized banks to cater the credit needs of agricultural farmers. The paper looks into the above-mentioned objectives by examining the trend of progress in the flow of agricultural credit from the formal financial institutions. Secondary data on trends in agro-rural credit outreach have been collected from various books, journals, magazines and web resources.

Provision of sufficient and timely credit at fair rates of interest has to be considered as an integral part of agricultural development. Assistance rendered by way of credit has, however, to be related to specific items of productive work or of essential costs of cultivation. In 1982, National Bank for Agriculture and Rural Development (NABARD) is the apex institution accredited with all matters concerning policy, planning and operations in the field of credit for agriculture and other economic activities in rural areas in India. NABARD serves as an apex refinancing agency for the institutions providing investment and production credit in rural areas.

The Concept of Micro-finance

Micro-finance has been defined as the provision of financial services (loans, savings, insurance and money transfers) to people excluded from the banking sector, is often invoked as the solution for financing agricultural farmers in rural India. But financing of small farms and .more broadly of the agricultural sector is difficult for numerous reasons. Banking institutions must face a variety of obstacles: insufficient infrastructure resulting in high transaction costs; covariance risks related to climate, price fluctuations and markets; lack of experience in evaluating the value of produce they are asked to finance; low education levels of fanners and farm labourers; and difficulties securing guarantees, to name but a few. Micro finance is powerful, but it is clearly no panacea. Agricultural loans are available for a multitude of farming purposes. Farmers may apply for loans to buy inputs for the cultivation of food grain crops as well as for horticulture, aquaculture, animal husbandry, and floriculture and sericulture businesses. There are also special loans to finance the purchase of agricultural machinery such as tractors, harvesters and trucks. Construction of biogas plants and irrigation systems as well as the purchase of agricultural land may also be financed through special types of agricultural finance. Micro-finance which includes, inter alia, micro credit and micro savings, is increasingly advocated by country planners to ensure timely and adequate credit to small and marginal farmers and to alleviate poverty. It is treated as an effective employment generator in rural areas having capability to sustain the income of the households by ensuring their opportunities to work. A preliminary analysis of the number of loans distributed through a high budgeted government-operated micro-finance programme, Swaraj ayati Gram Swarozgar Yojana (SGSY), by purpose, across the States in India indicates that 65 per cent of the total number of loans has been advanced to take up primary activities. The number of loans taken for service and secondary sectors is 15.3 and 19.7 per cent respectively. This revelation has provoked us to examine the implementation of this micro-finance programme and gauge its impact on the field level farmer clients. In this backdrop, this paper tries to review the trend, status and issues of agricultural credit in India and explores whether the present day formalization of informal micro-finance can increase universal access and bring in efficiency and cost effectiveness to loan financing in rural areas.

Here is some information about the kind of agricultural credit and loans provided by public sector banks in India. State Bank of India presents a wide range of financial schemes for agriculturalists. These schemes include crop loans, Produce Marketing Loan Scheme, Loan Against Warehouse Receipts, Kisan Credit Card Scheme, agricultural term loans, Land Development Scheme, Minor Irrigation Scheme, Farm Mechanisation Scheme, Financing of Combine Harvesters, Kisan Gold Card Scheme, Land Purchase Scheme, Krishi Plus Scheme, Arthias Plus Scheme, Dairy Plus Scheme, Broiler Plus Scheme, Finance To Horticulture, Lead Bank Scheme and Agri Business Heads Scheme. The Bank also provides Micro Finance through Self Help Groups and loans through 30 regional rural banks.

Schemes of Nationalized Banks

The Allahabad Bank

The bank offers the Kisan Credit Card and Kisan Shakti Yojana Scheme. The Kisan Credit Card is a unique scheme for farmers through which they can draw a cash loan for crop production as well as domestic needs from the card-issuing branch within the sanctioned limit. The Kisan Shakti Yojana provides farm investment credit, as well as personal/domestic loans including repayment of debt to moneylenders. The permissible loan limit will be 50 per cent of the value of land or 5 tunes the net farm income, whichever is lower.

Andhra Bank

The bank provides facilities to farmers like AB Kisan Vikas Card, AB Pattabhi Agricard, AB Kisan Chakra, rural godowns, agri clinics, agri service centres, self help groups and solar cookers. They also provide other schemes such as Kisan Sampathi, tractor financing, Kisan Green Card, Surya Sakhti and loans to dairy agents.

Bank of Baroda

The bank offers fanners the Baroda Kisan Credit Card. It also has schemes for the purchase of agricultural implements, heavy agricultural machinery like tractors, irrigation and other .infrastructure. Bank of Baroda also Finances the development of agri industries like horticulture, sericulture, fisheries, dairy and poultry.

Bank of India

It has a Kisan Credit Card Scheme that helps farmers raise short-term funds for agriculture and other farm-based activities, on an on-going basis, with very flexible and friendly repayment terms. It also offers an agricultural loan for development of agriculture related industries, purchase of machinery and other agricultural purposes.

Bank of Maharashtra

The bank offers agriculturists a Mahabank Kisan Credit Card and financial schemes for digging new wells, purchasing harvesters, livestock, vehicles and land. Repayment terms for different agricultural loans range from three to fifteen years.

Canara Bank

The bank provides Kisan Credit Cards. Limits up to 50,000 have no margin while those above 50,000 have a margin of 15 to 20 percent. Other than this, Canara Bank provides a wide array of financial schemes for different agricultural purposes.

Central Bank of India

The Central Kisan Credit Card is a credit service provided to farmers on the basis of their holdings for purchasing agricultural inputs. Only those farmers having a good track record for the past 2 years with the bank as a borrower or depositor and who are not defaulters to any credit institution would be considered for loans.

Corporation Bank

The bank offers a range of loan schemes to farmers. They are the Corp Gram Mitra Yojana, Corp Arthias Loan Yojana, Corp Kisan Tie-Up Loan Scheme, Corp Kisan Farm Mechanisation Scheme and Corp Kisan Vehicle Loan Yojna.

Dena Bank

Dena Bank has sponsored two Regional Rural Banks namely Dena Gujarat Gramin Bank in Gujarat and Durg Rajnandgaon Gramin Bank (DRGB) in Chhattisgarh. The bank has set up a Rural Development Foundation for training unemployed youth in rural areas. Other financial schemes of the bank are the Dena Swacch Gram Yojana, Dena Kisan Gold Credit Card Scheme and the Dena Bhumiheen Kisan Credit Card Scheme.

Indian Bank

It has a wide range of schemes for agriculturalists such as Swarojgar Credit Card, Gramin Mahila Sowbhagya Scheme, Kisan Bike Loan Scheme, Yuva Kisan Vidya Nidhi Yojana and Indian Bank Kisan Card Scheme.

Indian Overseas Bank

It offers agri-business consultancy services that include conducting feasibility and market studies, preparation of detailed project reports and formulation of rehabilitation packages for sick agro units.

Oriental Bank of Commerce

It has two agricultural projects the Grameen Project and the Comprehensive Village Development Programme. The Grameen Project involves disbursing small loans ranging from Rs. 75 onwards to mostly women. Training is also provided in villages in using locally available raw material to produce pickles and jams. The Comprehensive Village Development Programme focuses on providing an integrated package of rural finance to villagers to build up their village.

Punjab and Sindh Bank

The bank offers a range of financial schemes for farmers like the Zimidara Credit Card, tractor finance scheme, drip irrigation scheme, Kheti Udyog Khazana Yojana, vermi composting scheme, horticulture clinic and private veterinary clinic with dairy unit scheme.

Punjab National Bank

This bank has a special website called PNB Krishi for agriculturalists. It gives details on crop practices, plant protection, farm machinery, market prices and other farming news and activities. The website also provides a list of financial schemes offered by Punjab National Bank on production credit, investment credit, composite loans, animal husbandry and farm mechanization.

Syndicate Bank

The bank offers a wide range of agricultural loan products such as the Synd Jai Kisan Loan Scheme, Jewel Loan Scheme for Agriculture, Syndicate Farm House Scheme, Finance for Hi-tech Agriculture, Development of Irrigation Infrastructure scheme, Syndicate 2/3/4 Wheelers Scheme and the Syndicate Kisan Credit Card (S.K.C.C).

UCO Bank

This Bank provides the UCO Hirak Jayanti Krishi Yojana to meet the long-term credit needs of the farming community in rural areas for agriculture, allied activities as well as for personal purposes. Only farmers below 60 years are eligible to apply. Minimum quantum of the loan is Rs. 25,000 and the maximum is Rs. 5 lakhs.

Union Bank of India

It provided facilities to farmers include Kisan ATM Cards and special Kisan ATM Machines. These ATM's are easy to operate and do not require farmers to have a high level of literacy. They are vcice enabled in the local language, have a touch screen monitor and work on a biometric authentication system like finger print verification.

United Bank of India

The range of financial schemes offered to agriculturalists includes the United Krishi Laghu Paribahan Yojana, United Krishi Sahayak Yojana, United Gramyashree Yojana, Gramin Bhandaran Yojana and the United Bhumiheen Kisan Credit Card.

Vijaya Bank

This bank offers one comprehensive financial scheme known as the Vijaya Krishi Vikas (VKV) Scheme. This scheme provides a simple package to farmers to meet entire agricultural credit requirements such as crop production, investment credit and consumption credit. All farmers including owners, tenant cultivators, leased land farmers and sharecroppers are eligible for this scheme.

State Bank of India has signed separate agreements with Cargill, ITC, and National Agricultural Co-operative Marketing Federation among others for extending finance to farmers against warehouse receipts and for seed and crop cultivation, the bank said in a release. SBI has created a separate division to forge alliances with companies and government institutions to expand its farm loan business. "Similar MoUs with other leading corporate are under preparation in SBI. The banks already have tie-ups with 14 tractors, power tiller and combine harvester maker companies.

Conclusion

Micro finance is one of the few market-based, scalable anti-poverty solutions that are in place in India today and the argument to scale it up to meet the overwhelming need is compelling. It is considered by the government policy makers and banking experts as an important tool for sustainable development of Indian agricultural sector. Different innovative schemes have been invented and adopted by the banking sector to cater the micro credit needs of farmers that really help a lot for agricultural development in India. Specialized banking institutions have been established to cater the credk needs of Indian agricultural sector. A part of that the recovery of loans from farmers by these institutions is the need of an hour.

REFERENCES

Dutt Rudra & K.P.M. Sundharam, Indian Economy, S. Chand Publishers

http://india.gov.in/citizen/agriculture/schemes_incentives.php

http://www.vedamsbooks.com/no56650.htm

http://www.bouldermicrofinance.org/

http://www.agricultureinformation.com/mag

Khan MY (2007), *Indian Financial System* 5(e), Tata Mec-Graw Hill Company, New Delhi.

Ministry of Information & Broadcasting, Government of India-India 2007-Research, Reference and Training Division

News item(2006)Bank expands agri finance biz, financial *expressjul* 08.

Srivastava RM and Divya Nigam (2005); *Management of Indian Financial Institutions*, Himalaya Publishing House, New Delhi.

4

Finance by Primary Agriculture Co-Operative Bank: A Case Study

G. Chandrayya[1]
Dr. R.N. Misra[2]

Introduction

Agriculture plays a significant role in the economic development of India. Agriculture is the sources of livelihood for over 70 per cent of population in the country. To meet the requirements of the growing population and rapidly developing economy, agriculture has to grow fast and get modernized. This requires the use of high payoff inputs. Adoption of high yielding varieties require large quantities of fertilizers, plant protection chemicals, modernized equipments and machineries, which in turn, needs huge investment. The rural agricultural sector of the economy is labour-abundant, land poor and capital scarce. So it would be very difficult to get the benefits of modernisation of agriculture without adequate and timely supply of credit to the farmers.

Co-operative Credit Societies

Indian planners considered cooperative as an instrument of Economic development of the disadvantaged, particularly in the rural areas. They saw in a village panchayat, a village co-operative and a village school, as the trinity of institutions on which self reliant and just economic and social order was to

1 Lecturer in Commrce & Management Studies, Government College (A) Rajahmundry.
2 Prof. of PGCMS, SM IT, Berhampur.

be built. The non-exploitative character of co-operatives, voluntary nature of membership, the principle of one man one vote, decentralized decision making and self-imposed curbs on profits eminently qualified them as an instrument of development, combining the advantage of private ownership with public good.

The co-operative movement was started in India largely with a view to providing agriculturists funds for agricultural operations at low rates of interest and protect them from the clutches of money lenders.

Organisational Structure

The cooperative credit system in India is the largest in the world with 88,167 primary agricultural co-operative banks (PACB) at the village level, 353 central co-operative banks (CCB) at the district level and 28 state co-operative banks (SCB) at the State level. Thus the cooperatives have a three tier structure.

The SCB gets fund from NABARD (National Bank for Agricultural and Rural Development) and advances loans to the CCBs which in turn advance loans to the PACBs which are in direct touch with farmers.

Types of Credit

Short-term and medium term credits are provided by the co-operatives. Short-term credit having duration of less than 15 months is provided as crop loans, jewel loans and consumption loans. Crop loans are provided for the purpose of buying seeds, fertilizers, pesticides, etc. consumption loans help in purchasing durables. Medium-term loans with duration of 15 months to five years are provided for land improve ment, buying cattle agricultural implements and also for other industrial purposes. The scale of finance varies from different crops and purposes. The rate of interest varies according to the amount of loan and the purpose for which it is provided.

Though co-operatives are pioneers in providing credit to farmers, they suffer from the problem of over dues, seriously. This was reported by several past reports including the Khusro Committee of the Narasimhan committee.

The objectives of the study are

(*i*) To identify the factors influencing the demand for credit.

(*ii*) To assess the level of supply of credit for different purposes and factor influencing it.

(*iii*) To determine the extent of utilization of the credit provided by the bank.

(*iv*) To analyse the cases of defaults in repayment of loans with the view to identifying causes and remedies for them; and

(*v*) To suggest policy measures for revamping the primary agricultural cooperative Banks to best serve the fanners.

Scope and Methodology

Study of the demand for and supply of credit will help the bank to allocate more funds for major purposes for which they require funds and also provide adequate amount of funds at the right time. Study of the causes of default will provide lessons to the farmers on how to use credit in a better way for productive purposes so that they can repay the loan within the specified period. Examining the performance of the banks will help in identifying the difficulties involved in advancing and recovery of loans. This will enable the bank to alter their lending procedures and the repayment schedule. The study will help the policy makers to reformulate the policies so as to improve the performance of the banks.

Methodology

Sampling Procedure

The selected bank is performing successfully and had advanced loans for several purposes. Out of the 150 beneficiaries 50 are selected by lottery method and out of the 60 non-beneficiaries 25 samples are taken again by lottery method. The ultimate sample size is 75.

Period of Study

The study is undertaken during the months of December 2007 to February 2005 and primary data are collected for the agricultural year 2005-2007 and secondary data are collected for the agricultural years 2001-02 to 2006-07.

Limitations of the Study

The study is based largely on the primary data collected from the sample of farmers seeking co-operative credit and those who do not avail co-operative credit. As the farmers do not maintain any record for income and expenditure of the farm, particulars collected pertain to the memory of the farmers. Care was taken to reduce bias as far as possible. The study is limited to examining the performance of only one bank as the representative of the district, so generalization must be done with care.

Results and Discussions

The data collected from the sample farmers are analysed with reference to each of the specific objectives of the present study. It focused attention on the performance of PACE; demand for credit and supply of credit; factors influencing the supply of credit; credit gap of the farmers; problems faced by the farmers in availing loans and their own suggestions to solve them. The results are presented and discussed in this chapter. As a back-drop for discussion, knowledge of the socio-economic characteristics of the farmers would be helpful.

More specifically, the amount of credit demanded, supply of credit, credit gap and defaulting of loans are influenced by socio-personal characteristics of the borrowers. They include size of family, number of workers and experience of the farmers in farming, size of the farm, cropping pattern, cropping intensity, indebtedness of the farmers, farm income and borrowing from various sources. A comparison of these characteristics between the beneficiaries of PACE and nonbeneficiaries is presented.

Socio-Personal Characteristics

Some socio-personal characteristics that influence the decision making by the farmers are presented in Table-1. Majority of the beneficiary families (92 per cent) and non beneficiary families (80 per cent) have five and more than five members in the family.

Only eight per cent of the beneficiary households and 20 per cent of the non-beneficiary households have less than four members. Thus, large size is the characteristics of both beneficiary and non beneficiary farm families.

The number of workers in the family will decide the income of the family. In families benefited by the PACE the average number of working persons is 2.44 which is larger than that of the non-beneficiary families (2.20). The dependency ratio of the beneficiary families is 50.32 and for nonbeneficiary families is 40.14 per cent. Thus there are more workers and also relatively more dependents in the beneficiary families as compared to non-beneficiary families. Usually large number of dependents demanded more persons to go to work and PACE loans helped them.

Experience of the farmers in farming and allied activities would enable them to invest in more profitable enterprise appropriate to the season. The income of the farmers and the repayments of loans depend upon the experience of the farmers. Sixteen per cent of the beneficiaries has experience below five years and 12 per cent of the nonbeneficiaries has the same years experience. Beneficiaries with the same experience of *5-10* years and non-beneficiaries with the same experience form the next group. This is the large group. The number of beneficiaries and non-beneficiaries decrease as the years of experience increase. The fact that there is no such increasing dependency on the co-operatives for loans.

Size of Distribution of Farms

It is found that the average size of holding of beneficiary farms is 133.66 cents (1.34 acres) and of nonbeneficiary is only 127.76 cents (1.28 acres). Marginal farmers formed the largest group of both beneficiaries and non-beneficiaries. The average size of holding of the beneficiaries is 0.64 acres, 1.46 acres, 2.18 acres and 4.23 acres for the four sizes of groups.

The small farm with above 2.5 acres of land occupies 40.59 per cent of the total area.

Among the non beneficiaries, one marginal farm is operated in 34.78 per cent of the total area and nine marginal farms are operated in 65.21 per cent of the total area.

The size of farm influences the demand for and supply of credit. It could be observed that most of the beneficiary categories are marginal farmers and they do not have that much access to co-operative credit. Under the non-beneficiary also most of them are marginal farmers and that shows their dependence on other source of credit.

Cropping Pattern

The major crop cultivated by the beneficiaries and non-beneficiaries accounting for 49.85 per cent and 44.39 per cent of the gross cropped area respectively. For beneficiaries and non-beneficiaries, paddy is the second major crop. Coconut is grown in small area by both beneficiaries and nonbeneficiaries. Other crops represent and it occupies a very small area for cultivation.

Cropping Intensity

Cropping intensity would reveal the efficiency of land-use in crop production. Cropping intensity is the percentage of gross cropped area to the net area sown.

The cropping intensity of both beneficiaries and nonbeneficiaries was almost the same, largely because both worked under the same agro climatic conditions. This made the comparative study of the two groups meaningful.

Farm Income

An analysis of the income of the farm would show the credit worthiness of the farmers. It is observed in the analysis that the size of the average net income and average gross income of the beneficiaries are larger than those of non-beneficiaries.

Borrowings

The fanners borrowed from different sources such as co-operatives, commercial banks, and private money lenders.

The Co-operatives are the main source of finance contributing 59.90 per cent of the total borrowings of the beneficiaries followed by commercial banks. Commercial banks are the main source of borrowing for the non-beneficiaries contributing 62.30 per cent of the total borrowing followed by 37.70 per cent of borrowing from the private money-lenders. The borrowings of beneficiaries from the co-operatives are significantly larger due to their easy access to and low rate of interest. The beneficiaries depend on money-lenders also. That shows the less dependence on the co-operatives by the beneficiaries.

Indebtedness

Total amount of credit payable by a farmer measures the level of his indebtedness. It includes both amount of overdue and amount of outstanding for whatever purpose the loan was availed, difficult to calculate the demand for credit.

Credit Utilisation Pattern

One problem in borrowing by farmers from the PACE is the overdue caused by the misuse of the loans issued for productive puiposes.

Majority of the respondents (64 per cent) utilized the credit completely for the purpose for which it was taken and only 36 per cent has utilized the credit partially and diverted it. Regarding nonbeneficiaries, 68 per cent have used the loan from other sources to a maximum extent and 32 per cent made par tial utilization. There is the need for insisting on the use of productive loans fully for the purpose intended. The farmers should be encouraged on thrift, so that enough savings could be generated to meet the unforeseen expenses.

Reasons for Borrowing

The reasons for borrowing from cooperatives are given as follows. Twenty four per cent of the farmers stated easy accessibility and 76 per cent of the fanners stated low rate of interest. This is an indicator of good performance of the co-operatives.

Difficulties in Getting Loan

The difficulty in getting loan was due to the difficult procedures for 22 per cent, untimely loans for 1 8 per cent, security required for 24 per cent, problems in providing documents for 20 per cent and cost of availing loans for 16 per cent of the farmers. So the procedural formalities of the PACE need simplification. Short term loans are generally provided on the basis of personal security. Therefore, the reporting of providing security as a problem could be easily remedied.

REFERENCE

Babu, C.V., Inter-seasonal and Inter-farm Demand for production Credit and its Gap in Paddy Cultivation - A Micro Level Approach", *Agricultural Banker*, 15(5): 1992

Basavaraj Banker and S. Suryapradesh, "Credit Availability and its Impact on the Financial Position of the Farmers - A Case Study", *Agricultural banker*, 12(2): 1989.

Cole, G.D.H., Money: Its Present and Future, In: G.N. Singh and B.P. Sharma, *Agricultural Finance and Management*, Meerut: Friends Publications, 1990.

Des S.S.M. *Rural Banking in India* Bombay: Himalaya Publishing House, April 1983.

Dhingra. I.V. *Rural Banking in India*, New Delhi: Sultan Chand and Sons, 1987.

Fareeda, Khan. A *Commercial Lending for Agricultural Assets by Non-banking Financial Institutions – A Case Study for Aruna Sugars Finance limited – Madras,* Unpublished). M.B.M. Thesis,, Department of agricultural Economics, Tamil Nadu Agricultural University" Coimbatore, 1991.

Gandhimahi, *Performance of a Selected Nationalised Bank in India, Southern Economist*, 41(5). July 1,2002.

Geetha, Nagarajan, *Financing Agriculture: The Case of Muti-agency Credit Delivery System at Athoor Block, Madurai,* (Unpublished M.sc. (Ag) Thesis, Department of Agricultural Economics, Tamil Nadu Agricultural University coimbatore, 1 985).

Girija Shankar, G. and I.L. Srvastava. *Credit Availability and Requirements of FCV (Flue Cured Virgina) Tobacco – A Case Analysis in West Godavari District of Andhra Pradesh,* Agricultural Banker. 12(3): 1989.

Goyal, S.K., and R.N. Pandey, *An Analysis of Default of Crop Loan in Primary Agricultural Co-operative Credit and Service Societies in Haryana,* Agricultural Banker, 14(1): 1991.

Indira Sena Reddv. P, *Co-operative Banks for Agriculture and Rural Development – A Case Study*, Agricultural banker, 18(3): 1984.

Jery Josephine Jery. D. *A Study on the Industrial Development of Tuticorin,* 1994, An Unpublished Thesis, Y.,M.K. University.

John A. Hopkin, Peter J. Berry and C.B. Baker, *Financial Management in Agriculture,* (Illinois, The Interstate Printers and Publishers, Inc; 1973).

Joginder Singh and I.S. Chatha, *A Study of Magnitude of Farm Credit in Punjab*, Financing Agriculture, 22(2): 1990.

Kandasam LK.P., *Co-operative Loan Recovery in Periyar District of Tamil Nadu, Indian Co-operative Review,* 30(1): 1992.

Makadia J.J, B.L. Thumar and R. L. Shiyani, *An Evaluation of Acquisition and Utilization of Co-operative Review*, 30 (1): 1992.

Modi M.K. and K.N. Rai, *Estimation of Credit Need Among Farmers of District Kurukshetra, Haryana,* Agricultural Banker, 14(3): 1 991.

National Resource centre, Indian Cooperative Movement: A profile, New Delhi: National co-operative union of India, 1993.

Palanisamy. A, *Role of Co-operatives in Crop-loan – A study of the Konganapuram (salem St) Agricultural service co-operative Society,* Agricultural Banker, 11 (5): 1989.

Pandey. A.P, Agricultural Economics, S.S. Singh, T. Gupta and AK Gupta, *Handbook of Agricultural Sciences*, New Delhi: Kalyani publishers, 1994.

5

Agriculture Growth is the Road for the Development

T. Hymavathi Kumari[1]

The economy of India is as diverse as it is large, with a number of major sectors including manufacturing industries, agriculture, textiles and handicrafts, and services. Agriculture is a major component of the Indian economy. More than 75 % of our people have their livelihood as agriculture and agriculture-oriented works. Mahatma Gandhi said "Indian economy lives in rural villages", and many of the industries getting their raw material from agriculture sector.

The five Plans are give importance to the agriculture sector and rural development and rural people's employment. Land and water management systems were developed with an aim of providing uniform growth. Our agriculture sector achieved green revolution during 1970s after that we create white revolution in milk production. Despite some stagnation during the later modern era the policy makers was not concentrate the development of comprehensive agricultural program and rural development compare to urban development and industrial development. Nearly 21.1% of the entire rural population of India exists in difficult physical and financial predicament.

This particle focus on the present status of agriculture in India and the problems faced by the farmers and some

---

[1] Assistant Professor, Raghu Engineering College, Dakamarri, Visakhapatnam. E-mail ID:hymavathi.tenneti@gmail.com

suggestions to improve the productivity of agriculture sector in India.

Status of Agriculture in India

The Indian Agricultural sector provides employment to about 65% of the labour force, accounts for 27% of GDP, contributes 21% of total exports, and raw materials to several industries. The livestock sector contributes an estimated 8.4% to the country GDP and 35.85% of the agricultural output. India is the seventh largest producer of fish in the world and ranks second in the production of inland fish. Fish production has increased from 0.75 million tons in 1950-51 to 5.14 million tons in 1996-97, a cumulative growth rate of 4.2% per annum, which has been the fastest of any item in the food sector, except potatoes, eggs and poultry meat. However, there are still a host of issues that need to be addressed regarding Indian agriculture. Indian agriculture is heavily dependent on monsoons. The monsoons play a critical role in determining whether the harvest will be rich, average, or poor. The structural weaknesses of the agriculture sector are reflected in the low level of public investment, exhaustion of the yield potential of new high yielding varieties of wheat and rice, unbalanced fertilizer use, low seeds replacement rate, an inadequate incentive system and post harvest value addition.

Problems faced by the Agriculture Sector in India

Due to urbanization and industrialization use of agriculture land is reduced during the last one decade, agriculture lands are converted into residential houses and factories hence the number of agriculture labours lost their work and move to urban areas. This leads to low out put in agricultural products, insufficiency and rise in food articles prices. Number of surveys said that the world will go to face food insufficiency in near future. Current agricultural practices are neither economically nor environmentally sustainable and India's yields for many agricultural commodities are low. Poorly maintained irrigation systems and almost universal lack of good extension services are among the factors responsible. Fanners' access to markets is hampered by poor roads, rudimentary market infrastructure, and excessive regulation. In this perspective India is facing the following problems.

- The key problem of those dependent on agriculture, specially the poor, small and marginal farmers and weaker sections of the society, is finance. The traditional concern about accessibility of agricultural credit to the needy rural inhabitants is still alive even after increasing bank branch network, improving Co-operative Banking structure, evolving specialized rural banking institutions. There has been continuous decline in the five year plan outlays for agriculture is in Sixth Plan 5.8%, in Ninth Plan 4.9% and in Tenth Plan it is 3.9%.
- In India Maximum of landholders are fall under the category of Small farmers, so they are not able to meet out the increasing input cost and not able to introduce any new technological machineries in their farms due to low financial status.
- Infrastructure is also a significant factor in the process of development but country like our rural India has not posses the infrastructure such as roads, electricity, fertilizer and pesticides availability which caused the vulnerable damage to the growth of agriculture. While India has a wide network of rural finance institutions, many of the rural poor remain excluded, due to inefficiencies in the formal finance institutions, the weak regulatory framework, high transaction costs, and risks associated with lending to agriculture.
- Irrigation is key to agricultural production. Irrigation facilities are inadequate, as revealed by the fact that only 52.6% of the land was irrigated in 2003-04, which result in farmers still being dependent on rainfall, specifically the monsoon season. A good monsoon results in a robust growth for the economy as a whole, while a poor monsoon leads to a sluggish growth. The government must allocate funds to start the new irrigation projects to increase the cultivation.
- Low educational standards, socio-economic backwardness, inefficient and inadequate finance and

less marketing services are the main problems of agriculture sector.

In addition to the above mentioned problems there is a big problem facing by the farmers from financial institutions in India.

DISPARITIES IN BANK CREDIT DISPENSATION

Agriculture, which is the mainstay of 60% of people, received only 9% (Y-O-Y Aug 2007-08) of incremental bank credit as against 13% during 2006-07. And only 6% of it goes to farmers as direct finance. Credit to industry increased from 40% to 45%. The ratio of agricultural credit to agricultural GDP was only 33% at end-March 2007 whereas the ratio of industrial credit to industrial GDP was a whopping 94%. The mandated lending to agriculture, 18% of net bank credit was never achieved since 1990s (reforms period).

Measures to Improve Agriculture Productivity

- Agricultural reforms and increased private investment is must, especially small farmers. Create a viable model of public-private partnership that allows private investors to invest in agriculture infrastructure in partnership with banks and financial institutions. This will help the farmers to access the high quality technologies and increase the output with international standards to meet the global market requirements.
- Agricultural research is required to adopt new technologies in the production process to improve productivity.
- Improving Water Resource and Irrigation/Drainage Management: Increase in multi-sectored competition for water highlights the need to formulate water policies and unbundled water resources management from irrigation service delivery.
- Improving the performance of rural financial institutions like RRB's and Rural Credit Co-operatives by enhancing regulatory measures such as improving the legal

framework for loan recovery collateral securities. It should increase micro finance to the rural public.

- The average size of land holdings is very small (less than 20,000 m^2) and is subject to fragmentation, due to land ceiling acts and in some cases, family disputes. Such small holdings are often over-manned, resulting in disguised unemployment and low productivity of labour.
- The fact that the regulated market Acts had been enacted to ensure that farmers do not get exploited by the money lenders, and that if produce was brought to the regulated markets, it would be possible for the state procurement agencies to pick up bulk quantities has been conveniently forgotten. The Indian farmer today does not need protection. . . he needs freedom. . . the freedom to buy and sell his commodities to whomsoever he wants to. . . .He wants to the freedom to export his commodities - be they onions or basmati rice to the market, which gives him the best offering. Unfortunately, given domestic policy constraints, and the sensitivity of the newspaper reading public to the price of onions and milk, in times of a demand supply mismatch, the government intervenes in favour of the urban consumer, which is more vocal.

Conclusion

It is the time to improve agriculture sector in India by introducing sophisticated technologies by providing financial support to the farmers of low income groups. The policy makers in India have a high responsibility on reducing poverty by raising agricultural productivity and developing the rural population economic status from deprived condition. However, bold action from policymakers will be required to shift away from the existing subsidy-based regime that is no longer sustainable, to build a solid foundation for a highly productive, internationally competitive, and diversified agricultural sector. It is evidently proved that the development of the nation especially a country like India depends on the agriculture sector only.

REFERENCES

Khan MY (2007), *Indian Financial Systems,* Tata McGraw-Hill Company, New Delhi.

Srivastava, RM and Divya Nigam (2005), *Management of Indian Financial Institutions,* Himalaya Publishing House, New Delhi.

Reserve Bank of India (2006), *Hand book of Statistics on the Indian Economy, Mumbai.*

Rindos, David (1984): *The Origins of Agriculture: An Evolutionary Perspective* Academic Press.

6

Institutional Finance to Agricultural Sector—A Study

Prabin Kumar Padhy,[1]
Dr. R.N. Mishra[2]

Introduction

Agriculture is an important occupation and mainstay of Indian Population. It supplements 26% of our GDP. More than 60% of Indian population are depending directly and indirectly on agriculture. Out of 30 districts of the State of Orissa, we have taken, Ganjam District as sample district. Ganjam district contributes a lion's share in the agricultural map of Orissa. For the purpose of our study only secondary data are taken into consideration, so all the limitations of secondary data are applied here. The growth and development of agriculture out of various factors timely, adequate finance is highly essential. Unless proper finance has been provided by the institutional agencies and the use of fund by the borrowers are considered most important in the growth and development of agriculture sector in the country as well as in the State of Orissa.

Institutional finance is divided into five types

(*i*) Crop Loan for transplantation, weeding out the grass from the field, harvesting the crop, improvement in the fertility of the soil

[1] H.O.D., Faculty of Management, GIST Berhampur, Orissa.
[2] Prof. MBA PGCMS, SMIT, Berhampur, Orissa.

(*ii*) Agriculture term loan for removing the layer of the soil and putting a new layer of the soil, leveling the land, buying agriculture implements like tractor, combined harvestor

(*iii*) Allied to agriculture - in this some secondary occupation is undertaken like fishing, poultry, horticulture, forestry, lumbering

(*iv*) Non-Farm services It consisted of Service Sector, Small Scale Industries, Agro Industries and

(*v*) Other Priority Sector All the other sectors of agriculture are considered as other priority sector. Institutional finance by different institutions is explained Table 6.1.

Whether agriculture or industry finance is considered as the lifeblood. There are three types of finance viz Short-term finance, Medium term finance, and Long-term finance. In 2006-07, total agricultural finance in India was 571 crores, it rose to 659 crores in 2007-08 giving rise in finance of 15.41% over the previous year. Further in 2008-09 agricultural finance rose to 693 crores resulting a rise of 5.15%. The total agricultural finance may be for different sector. If we study sector-wise in 2006-07 the crop Loan was 267 crores, it rose to 279 crores in 2007-08 resulting a rise of 11.1% over the past year. In 2008-09 it went to 297 crores with a rise of 6.45% over the previous year.

Agricultural Term Loan was 41 crores in 2006-07. It enhanced to 55 crores in 2007-08 resulting a growth rate of 24.14% in agricultural finance. The same trend was also maintained in 2008-09. In allied to agriculture in 2006-07, 42 crores finance was extended. It enhanced to 5.9 crores in 2007-08 resulting a growth rate of 40.4% over the past year.

In non-farm sector in 2006-07, 37 crores finance was given. It went up to 54 crores in 2007-08 resulting a growth rate of 45.9% over the last year. It has been further enhanced to 69 crores in 2008-09 giving rise of 27.77% over the previous year.

In other priority sector in 2006-07, finance was extended to the extent of 184 crores. It enhanced to 212 crores resulting an increase of 15.2% over the previous year. It rose further to 215 crores resulting a growth rate of 1.41% over the previous year.

Table 6.1. Institutional Finance to Agriculture in India Borad Sectorwise comparison of Finance to Agriculture by Financial Institutions in India in 2006-07, 2007-08, 2008-09

Sector	*2006-07 (in crores)*	*2007-08 (in crores)*	*Increase / decrease (crores)*	*% of increase / decrease*	*2007-08 (crores)*	*2008-09 (crores)*	*Increase / decrease (crores)*	*% of increase / decrease*
Crop Loan	267	279	12	4.49	279	297	18	6.45
Agricultural Term Loan	41	55	14	34.15	55	55	00	0.00
Allied to Agriculture	42	59	17	40.48	59	57	-02	3.39
Non farm Sector	37	54	17	45.95	54	69	15	27.77
Other Priority Sector	184	212	28	15.22	212	215	03	1.42
Total	571	659	88	15.41	659	693	34	5.167

Source: Annual Credit Plan, (2006-09) pp. 64-70.

Agriculture Finance by Different Banks

There are 30 institutions in public sector as well as private sector providing credit to agricultural farmers of different types in Ganjam District. The credit providing to farmers are in different field namely crop loan, agricultural term-loan, Non-Farm Services, Allied to agriculture etc. Out of the total finance in 2008-09, 75% of finance are provided by Commercial Banks. The premier financial assistance is provided to agriculture is State Bank of India (19.50%), Rushikulya Gramya Bank (19.01%), Aska Central Cooperative Bank (12.73%), The Berhampur Central Cooperative Bank (12.28%), Andhra Bank (10.52%). Of the total finance 38,051 lakhs in the year 2008-09 in the Ganjam District of the State of Odisha.

Finance by State Bank of India in Ganjam District

Agricultural Finance is extended by Commercial Banks, Regional Rural Banks, Co-operative Banks and and Orissa State Financial Corporation. Out of the above, I have selected State Bank of India for the purpose of the study. We have taken agriculture finance by State Bank of India in Ganjam District. Due to constraints of time and unavailability of resources and heavy

Table 6.2. Broad Sectorwise comparison of credit allocation of Ganjam District under Priority Sector advances in 2006-07, 2008-09 by State Bank of India

Sector	*2007-08 (lakhs)*	*2008-09 (lakhs)*	*Increase / Decrease (lakhs)*	*Percentage*
Crop Loan	2970.17	3067.50	97.33	3.28
Agricultural Term Loan	1121.59	1090.41	-131.18	-10.74
Allied to agriculture	1136.06	1432.33	296.27	26.08
Non-Farm Sector	879.33	1583.10	703.77	80.03
Total	12354.72	13515.77	1161.05	9.40

Source : Annual Credit Plan. (2006-09), pp 64-70.

rainfall in the Coastal districts, it was not possible to collect information timely. So, I am depicting out agricultural finance in Ganjam District by State Bank of India. Agricultural Finance in Ganjam District for the year 2007-08 and 2008-09 is explained in Table 6.2.

In 2007-08, total agricultural finance by all financial institutions extended in Ganjam District was 65,918 lakhs and in 2008-09 the same has increased to 69,298 lakhs with a rise of 5.12% over the previous year. I observed State Bank of India is the largest financier providing 18.74% of agriculture finance in 2007-08 in Ganjam district. It went up to 19.5% of total finance in 2008-09 in Ganjam district.

If we discuss sectorwise, crop loan was 2970.17 lakhs in 2007-08 in Ganjam district. It rose to 3067.50 lakhs in 2008-09 with a rise of 97.33 lakhs over the previous year with 3.28% rise in agricultural finance.

In allied to agriculture the finance extended was 1136.06 lakhs in 2007-08 in Ganjam district by State Bank of India. It enhanced to 1432.33 lakhs in 2008-09 with a rise of 296.27 lakhs over the previous year with a growth rate of 26.07% over the previous year.

In Non-farm services finance extended was 879.33 lakhs in 2007-08. It rose to 1583.10 lakhs in 2008-09. There is a rise of 703.77 lakhs over the previous year with a 80.03% rise over the previous year.

In other Priority Sector finance disbursed was 61147.57 lakhs in 2007-08. It extended to 6342.43 lakhs in 2008-09 with a rise of 194.86 lakhs over the previous year with a rise of 3.17% over the previous; year.

Suggestions for Remedial Solutions to Overcome the Present Crisis of the Farming Community

(1) The farmers are not getting remunerative price to leave any surplus after meeting their livelihood. So, the government has to increase procurement price of paddy, wheat, pulses and all farming produce.

(2) Hybridization and supply of high yielding varieties of seeds are to be supplied to the farmers to double and

treble their yield. Seed banks should; be opened in the village panchayats, well equipped with the availability of seeds all the time to ensure improvement in agriculture practices.

(3) Old fashioned cultivation practices should be replaced by new and scientific methods of cultivation. All agricultural practices should be supplemented by tractors and combined harvester's mechanization. The cooperative farming should be introduced among the farmers to increase production and productivity.

(4) Rampant Corruption among the Government officials and bank officials for financing agriculture. The subsidy remains on record only, the major portion of agriculture finance including subsidy is eaten up by Officials of the bank and Revenue Department. Only a little portion of the benefit reaches the farmers. So this is a major obstacle in agriculture finance has to be removed at the outset.

(5) Commercialization of agriculture including contract buying should be introduced in agriculture and Corporate Sector should come forward in this area to exploit.

(6) Callousness of the Government and apathetic attitude possessed by Government department to provide agriculture finance.

(7) Crop Insurance should be provided to all the farmers free of cost to all the farmers irrespective of the size of the land and category of the farmers for natural calamity like drought, heavy rainfall etc.

(8) Seasonal unemployment of the farmers should be removed by providing good irrigational facilities round the year to remove laziness among the farmers.

(9) Last but not the least collection centres should be opened in village panchayats for collecting the produce of the farmers so that farmers will get a price of their produce and instant payment should be done or the amount should be credited to their bank amounts to free the

farmers from the clutches of mill owners and touts who are simply grabbing the produce of the farmers by paying meager price and fleecing them.

REFERENCES

Annual Credit Plan 2005-06.

Annual Credit Plan 2006-07.

Annual Credit Plan 2007-08

Annual Credit Plan 2008-09.

Annual Report of State Bank of India 2006-07.

Annual Report of State Bank of India 2007-08.

Annual Report of State Bank of India 2008-09.

7

Institutional Finance and Recoveries

Dr. H. Srinivas Rao[1]

Introduction

In the modern era also Indian farming is much dependent on ramrail only. Nobody is able to predict the degree of rainfall perfectly because of which many small farmers and medium range forming community is loosing not only their fortunes but also their invested capital.

Agriculture farmers in rural areas much depend on unorganized financing facilities offered by money lenders and indigenous bankers at an abnormal rate.

Since independence, central and state governments have initiated several agricultural credit financing schemes/ programmes to farming of community under the institutional credit financing banner. However progress achieved by this is very limited.

Objectives of the Study

In this direction, an attempt is made here to study the extent of institutional finance to farming community in one hand, and the degree of recovery on the other hand, further an attempt also be made to draw the conclusions emerging out of the present study and offer few suggestions to strengthen the institutional credit and recovery system.

[1] Sr. Lecturer in Commerce, Badruka College of Commerce, Kachiguda, Hydrabad-27.

Data and Methodology

For the purpose of present study secondary data are collected from different published sources and suitable-tabulated, analyzed.

Needs for Credit for Indian Farmers

The financial requirements of the Indian farmers can be classified into three types depending upon the period and the purpose for which they are required :

(*a*) Farmers need funds for short periods of less than 15 months for the purpose of cultivation or for meeting domestic expenses. For example, they want to buy seeds, fertilizers, fodder for cattle, etc. They main require funds to support their families in those years when the crops have not been good or adequate for the purpose. Such short - period loans are normally repaid after the harvest.

(*b*) The farmers require finances for medium period ranging between 15 months and 5 years for the purpose of making some improvement on land, buying cattle, agricultural implements, etc. These loans are larger than short-terms loans and can be repaid over longer periods of titise.

(*c*) The farmers need finances for the purpose of buying additional land, to make permanent improvement on land, to pay off old debt and lo purchase costly agricultural machinery. These loans are for long periods of more than 5 years.

We can further classify the credit requirements of farmers into two types - productive and unproductive loans. The former include loans to buy seeds, fertilizers, implements, etc. to pay taxes to the Government and lo make permanent improvements on land, such as digging and deepening of wells, fencing of land. etc.

Sources of Rural Credit

Broadly, there are two sources of credit available to the farmers -institutional and private. Non-institutional or private sources include money-lenders, traders and commission agents, relatives and landlords institutional sources consist of the Government and co-operatives, commercial banks including the Regional Rural Banks (RRBs).

Non-institutional sources - money-lenders, landlords, traders. Accounted for 93 per cent of the total credit requirements in 1951-52 and institutional sources including the Government accounted for only 7 per cent of the total credit needs in that year. The All India Debt and Investment Survey (1981) estimated that the share of non-institutional sources had slumped to about 37 per cent in 1981, money-lenders accounting for barely 16 percent; the share of institutional credit, however, had jumped lo 63 percent - co-operatives contributing 30 per cent and commercial banks about 29 per cent.

H.T. IIEF Study on Rural Credit (2004)

The Hindustan Times (HT) and Invest India Economic Times (HEF) using IRES data (2004) has brought outstartling facts about earners, who use money-lenders as the source of credit. The study has revealed the following facts :

1. The share of various sources in rural credit by earners reveals that the share of moneylender in total credit is 70 percent. In absolute terms, it of the order of Rs. 67,000 crores. The share of public sector banks is 10 percent, followed by co-operative societies at 9 per cent. The share of self-help groups (SHGs) is one per cent. Government loans also account for barely 1 percent and other sources account for 9 per cent (Table 7.1).
2. Forty six Million earners use money lenders and nearly half of them reside in some of the richest states including Andhra Pradesh, Karnataka, Tamil Nadu, Maharashtra and Gujarat.
3. Majority of the borrowers are farmers (32%) or agricultural or wage labourers (39%). Nearly 3.7 million customers of moneylenders are regular salaried employees. Another 7.36 million earn over Rs. 60,000 while 3.6 million of them are taxpayers.

4. Increasingly, nearly 88 percent of all moneylender customers can access a government credit programme within one kilometer from their homes while 30 percent have access to SHGs. However, 29 million earners prefer to use moneylenders for their credit needs.

Table 7.1. Share of different agencies in Rural Credit (2004)

Agency	*Share in total Credit (%)*
Money-lenders	70
Public Sector Banks	10
Co-Operatives Banks and Societies	9
Governments Loans	1
Self-help Groups (SHGs)	1
Others	9
Total	100

Source: Hindustan Times- IIEF Study (2004).

5. Moneylenders charge an average interest of 24 per cent per annum compared to 12 percent by nationalized PSU banks and cooperative banks. Even then, 70 per cent of customers avail of the credit of moneylenders.
6. Average outstanding credit from all sources is Rs. 22,910 of this, the moneylender hold an average credit of Rs. 14,610 *i.e.,* nearly 64 percent.

Obviously, the hold of moneylenders in total rural credit has bounced back to 70 per cent and PSU banks and cooperative banks have trailed behind at merely 19 percent. This shows the failure of the institutional credit to meet the needs of farmers, landless labourers and wage earners in rural India.

CREDIT DELIVERY MECHANISM IN RURAL FINANCE MULTI-AGENCY APPROACH

Need for Institutional Finance

The need for institutional credit arises because of the weakness or inadequacy of private agencies to supply credit to farmers.

Private credit is defective because:

(*i*) It is based on profit motive and, therefore it is always exploitative.

(*ii*) It is very expensive and is not related to the productivity of land.

(*iii*) It does not flow into most desirable channels and to most needy persons.

(*iv*) It is not available for making agricultural improvements - and much of the necessary improvements are not undertaken as funds are not available for long periods at low rates of interest and

(*v*) It is not properly integrated with the agriculturists other needs.

Institutional credit is not exploitative and the basic motive is always to help the farmer to raise his productivity and maximise his income. The rate of interest is not only relatively low but can be different for different groups of farmers and for different purposes. Institutions also make a clear distinction between short-term credit and long-term credit requirements and give loans accordingly. Finally, institutional credit is fully integrated with other needs of agriculturists. The farmers require not only credit but also guidance in the planning of their agricultural operations like the use of seeds, fertilizers pesticides etc., assistance in raising crops and in general, help for maximizing their income. Agricultural credit and agricultural improvement should go hand in hand and the farmers should be taught improved farming methods and also be provided adequate and cheap credit. In all developed countries, provision of credit facilities and extension services go hand in hand. This work can be done best by institutions like cooperative societies and commercial banks and not by rapacious money lenders and commission agents.

National Policy and Objectives

Since independence, *a multi-agency approach* consisting of cooperative, commercial banks and regional rural banks known as institutional credit has been adopted to provide cheaper and adequate credit to farmers. The major policy in the sphere of agricultural credit has been its progressive institutionalization for supplying agriculture and rural development progrmmes with adequate and timely flow of credit to assist weaker sections and less developed regions.

The basic objectives of this policy are :

(*a*) To ensure timely and adequate flow of credit to the farming sector,

(*b*) To reduce and gradually eliminate the moneylenders from the rural scene,

(*c*) To make available credit facilities to all the regions of the country *i.e.,* reduce regional imbalances and,

(*d*) To provide larger credit support to areas covered by special programmes like Pulses Development Programmes. Special Rice Production Programme and the National Oilseeds Development Project.

Institutional credits as mentioned earlier, refers to the funds made available by co-operative societies, commercial banks, and Regional Rural Banks (RRBs).

Evolution of Multi-agency Approach

Faced with the serious problem of deteriorating agricultural production and the rapacious money lenders, the Government set up cooperative credit societies and land mortgage banks. Much was expected from the cooperative credit movement as it was led by the farmers themselves. A survey of rural credit in 1950-51 showed that the co-operative could meet barely 3.3 per cent of the total credit requirements of farmers, while the money lenders accounted for 93 per cent of the credit needs of the farmers. The All-India Rural Credit Survey Committee (1954) state: "co-operation has failed, but co-operation must succeed". On the recommendations of this committee, Reserve Bank of India took a series of measures to strengthen the co-operative movement.

The State Bank of India was set up in 1955 to show, among other things, a special concern for agricultural credit. It was the All Indian Rural Credit Survey Committee (1969) which recommended the adoption of "multi agency approach" to finance the rural sector. For the first time, the Government openly accepted that rural credit could not be met by co-operative societies alone and that commercial banks should play an important role in the rural sector. This was a basic reason for the taking over of 14 leading banks in 1969. This was followed by the setting up of Regional Rural Banks (RRBs). Thus, the multi-agency approach of institutional credit to agriculture was evolved over a number of years.

While Recerve Bank of India was helping the co-operative sector directly, it was felt that the multi-agency approach to rural finance required a special banking institution to coordinate and help all the institutions specializing in rural finance. It was for this reason that NABARD was set up as the apex hank for rural finance in 1982.

Institutional Credit to Agriculture

In June 2004, the government announced a credit package for the agricultural sector, which envisaged doubling of agricultural credit over a period of three year. The target for growth of agricultural credit for the year 2004-05 was kept at 30 per cent. This target was exceeded as the actual growth in overall credit by all agencies was as high as 44 percent (from Rs. 86,981 crore in 2003-04 to Rs. 1,25,309 crore in 2004-05). Based on this encouraging performance, the target for flow of institutional credit for agriculture and allied activities for 2005-06 was raised to Rs. 1,41,000 crore which was again surpassed by the actual achievement of Rs. 1,80,486 crore. In the Budget for 2006-07 the Finance Minister laid down the target for agricultural credit for this year at Rs. 1,75,000 crore. In a bid to provide more and cheap credit to farmers, the government also reduced the interest rate on short-term credit to farmers form 9 percent to 7 per cent on loans of less than Rs. 3 lakh. The banks were also asked to add 50 lakh more farmers to their portfolio. The target laid down for the year 2006-07 was also exceeded as the agricultural credit during this year Rs. 2,03,297 crore. This shows that the target of doubling agricultural credit in a period of three years was surpassed and the actual achievement has been much more. In the Union Budget for 2007-08, the Finance

Minister proposed a target of Rs. 2,25,000 crore (again higher than the target). The banks were asked to add 50 lakh new farmers to their portfolio, target for agricultural credit for the year 2008-09 was kept at Rs. 2,80,000 crore. The two percent interest subvention scheme proposed for short-term loans in the 2006-07 budget has been continued in 2007-08, 2008-09 and 2009-10.

Table 7.2. Institutional Credit to Agriculture : Relative Share of Different institutions

(Per cent)

Year	*Co-operatives Bank*	*Scheduled Commercial*	*Regional Rural Bank*	*Total Credit to Agriculture*
1970-71	100.0	-	-	744
1980-81	61.6	38.4	-	3,292
1990-91	49.0	47.6	3.4	9,830
2000-01	39.4	52.6	8.0	52,827
2001-02	38.0	54.1	7.9	62,045
2002-03	34.1	57.2	8.7	69,560
2003-04	31.0	60.3	8.7	86,981
2004-05	25.0	65.0	10.0	1,25,309
2005-06	21.8	69.7	8.5	1,80,486
2006-07	20.9	69.1	10.0	2,03.297

Source : Indian Economy pp. 300 from Himalya Publications,

Recovery Performance

A variety of factors influence the levels of and the trends in the overdues. It is difficult to pinpoint a single cause as responsible for overdues. Various factors are responsible for overdues, even though the degree of influence of each factor may differ from case to case. It can only be said that no single factor, but a combination of different factors would be at play in the recovery operations of a bank which cumulatively determine the trends in the overdues.

Common Causes of Overdues

The various official and non-official studies on the problem of overdues bring out the following as common causes of overducs at the farmer level :

1. Failure of crops due to drought, cyclone, hailstorm, pests and erratic supply of power. Certain parts of the State are on and off subject to cyclones and droughts.
2. Infractions investment - wells failing to strike water, or death of livestock financed.
3. Delays in sanction and disbursements of loans and thereafter lack of/inadequate supportive service facilities such as production loans/consumption loans, required by the borrowers for making optimum use of borrowed funds and also some times leading to diversion/ misutilisation of loan funds.
4. Flucturating yields and increasing cost of agricultural production, further accentuated by uneconomic unstable prices leading to inadequate surplus.
5. Financial in discipline at all levels both on the part of borrowers and lenders.
6. Wilful default *i.e.,* though a loanee has the capacity to pay his loan instalment he avoids payment intentionally.

Conclusions

The following conclusions are emerged from the present study :

1. The extent of institutional credit for farmers in recent years shows that total agricultural credit from institutional sources had steadily increased from Rs. 6,230 crores in 1984- 85 to Rs. 62,040 crorcs in 2001-02 and is likely to exceed Rs. 80,000 crores in 2003-04.
2. Different forms of credit help the farmers in their agricultural operation are in proving there land. Besides these in the Indian formers often borrow for unproductive purposes too, such as for celebration of marriages, births and deaths for litigation etc.,

Unproductive loans raised at exorbitant rates of interest are highly improper and unjustified.

3. In recent years the share of non-institutional sources for credit financing is declining at a faster rate due to State and Central Governments proactive actions in rural credit expansions programmes.
4. Access to and knowledge of cheaper alternative credit sources have not dampened the demand of money-lenders. This is not due of lack of information but other factors like procedural delays and lack of promptness by institutional credit as compared to easy and prompt delivery moneylender.
5. The institutional credit flow to agriculture during the Ninth Plan period (1997-2002) was Rs. 2,30,000 crores for the five-year period the average credit flow per annum was Rs. 4,6000 crores. The Tenth Plan (2002-07), however, has projected a substantial jump in institutional credit flow to the agricultural sector to the tune of Rs. 7,36,600 cores almost three times, as compared to the Ninth Plan) -and the annual average credit flow would be Rs. 1,49,120 crores.
6. The total institutional credit to agriculture, has been steadily rising, there has been :
   (*a*) steady decrease in percentage terms, in the contribution of cooperative banks in rural credit from 55% in 1984 to 25% in 2004-05.
   (*b*) the share of RRBs is almost insignificant between 6 per cent to 10 per cent.
   (*c*) the share of commercial banks has been steadily rising from 45 per cent to 65 per cent in 2004-05. It would be a good idea if cooperative banks and RRBs are made subsidiaries.

Suggestions

(*i*) To step agricultural credit form a all lending institutions cooperative banks, RRBs and commercial banks (30 percent increase - this will continue year after year).

(*ii*) The branches of commercial banks and RRBs will be energized to enhance the flow of agricultural credit.

(*iii*) Under special agriculture credit plan, at least 100 new farmers should be financed at each rural and semi - urban branch during 2004-05, resulting in 50 percent lakh new farmers.

(*iv*) Financing of at least 2 to 3 new investment projects by each branch in plantations and horticulture, fisheries, organic farming, etc.

(*v*) Providing credit to tenant farmers and oral lessees.

(*vi*) Debt restructuring as opposed to debt write off in the following forms:

(*a*) Relief to farmers in distress by rescheduling their loans and making them eligible for fresh loans and

(*b*) One-time settlement for small and marginal farmers and consider them eligible for fresh loans.

REFERENCES

Co-operative Banking in New Millennium, Anmol Publications.

Indian Economy, Himalya Publications.

Indian Economy, S. Chand Publications.

8

Institutional Finance to Agriculture Sector in Orissa

Sri S.K. Badatya,[1]
Dr. R.N. Mishra[2]

The Republic of India is a vast country. It account for 16 per cent of the world's population, but has only 2.4 per cent share in the land surface of the world. In a relative sense, India's position in this respect is distinctly unfavourable. In terms of geographical area, India ranks seventh among the countries of the world after Russia, U.S.A., Canada, China, Brazil and Australia. India's area is one-seventh of that of Russia and one-third of that of the U.S.A., Canada and China. But no less important is the fact that; the geographical area of India is quite large 328.7 million sq. ha from the snow covered Himalayan heights to tropical rain forest of the South.

The natural resources of a country are of primary importance for the economic development. As a matter of fact natural resources determine. the economic life of a nation. The U.S.A. is both an agricultural as well as industrial country but Japan is an industrial country only because there is no scope for agriculture as the very nature of the soil is not favourable for agriculture. India has been known as an agricultural country. Eighty per cent of its population resides in the villages and only 20 per cent lives in the urban area. Agriculture forms the backbone of Indian economy despite the concentrated

---

[1] Faculty Member, MBA, SMIT, Berhampur, Orissa.
[2] Professor, MBA, SMIT, Berhampur, Orissa.

industrialized during the Plan period, agriculture still occupies a pride of places. It is important sector of Indian economy. In India in the year 1950-51 the per centage share of agriculture and Allied activities in Gross Domestic Product(GDP) was 59.2 per cent but it has been declined to 22.9 per cent in the year 2004-05. In the year 1950-61 the per centage share of agricultural exports was about 44 per cent of the total exports whereas in the year 2004-05 it was reduced to 10.2 per cent.

Agriculture is the mainstay of Orissa economy providing livelihood support to large sections of the populations. It constitute 20.09 per cent of net domestic product of the State in 2007-08 and provide employment directly, indirectly to around 70 per cent of the total workforce. Development of agriculture is Orissa has lagged behind due to several constraints like traditional method of cultivation, inadequate capital formation and low investment, inadequate irrigation facilities and uneconomic size of holding. For sustaining economic development, much emphasis has been laid down in the planning of accelerating the pace of agricultural development by taking steps to expanding irrigation facilities, extending supply of credit, remove regional imbalances in cropping pattern, evolving new verities of seeds and also providing support to farmers.

Agricultural credit is an essential input for augmenting agricultural production and helping the poverty stricken farmers of Orissa in meeting their investment requirements. Against the target of Rs.3738.57 crores, an amount of Rs.3657.28 crores of agricultural loan have been advances during 2007-08 showing an achievement of 97.38 per cent which is 10.23 per cent higher than the agricultural loan advanced during 2006-07 out of the total agricultures loan financed during 2007-08 the share of Co-operative Banks was 44.42 per cent Commercial Banks 41.39 per cent and Regional Rural Bank 14.19 per cent respectively.

Objectives of the Study

The basic objectives of the present study are as follows:-

1. To analyze the performance of financial institutions in financing to agricultural sectors in Orissa during the study period.

2. To examine the share of agriculture sector in financing to other sectors in Orissa.

Scope and Limitation of Study

The different banks in Orissa played very important role in financing agricultural sector in Orissa. For the purposes of the study only secondary data are taken for the year 2002-03 to 2007-08 so all the limitations of secondary data are found in the study.

Methodology

The study is based on secondary data collected from the various economic surveys of Orissa. The period of study chosen covers 2000-01 to 2007-08. The indicator selected for studying the performance of financial institution in financing to agricultural sector and also made comparative study in financing to other sectors in Orissa. For evaluation of the performance, the ratios and per centages have been computed using the data on the various economic surveys of Orissa.

Analysis and Discussion: Agricultural Credit

Like all other producers, the farmers also require credit, "credit supports the farmers as the hangman's rope supports the hanged". That agriculturist cannot carry on his business without outside finance is a fact proved by history and evidenced by the poverty and indebtedness of the persons engaged in the business of agriculture. Agricultural credit is an essential input for augmenting agricultural productions and helping the poverty stricken formers of Orissa in meeting their investment requirement.

Table 8.1 shows us the details of finance made by financial institutions to agricultural sector in Orissa for the period 2002-03 to 2007-08. It can be observed from the table that the total funds sanctioned increases every year from 2002-03 to 2007-08 of Rs.1046.55 crore to 3657.28 crores respectively which is equal to 349 per cent. The total funds financed to agricultural sector for the period 2002-03 to 2007-08 is Rs.13,953.40 crores. Out of this share of Co-operative Bank's is 7923.52 crores(49.8 per cent) fallowed by Commercial Banks Rs. 5379.91 crores (35.30 per cent) & RRB is 2342.66 crores(14.90 per cent). The total amount of agricultural loans advanced by different commercial banks, RRB, cooperative banks and OSFC during 2004-05 was to the tune of 3657.28 cores which was higher by 10.23 per cent as compared 3317.95 cores financed in 2006-07. Out of total agricultural loan financed during 2007-08 the share of cooperate banks was 44.42 per cent fallowed by 41.39 per cent commercial banks, 14.18 per cent by RRBs.

Table 8.1. Agricultural credit advanced by financial institution in Orissa from 2002-03 to 2007-08

Year	*Commercial Banks*	*RRB*	*Cooperative Banks*	*OSFC*	*Total*
2002-03	281.4	15589	609.00	0.26	1046.55
2003-04	438.89	167.65	724.03	0.31	1326.88
2004-05	627.89	304.66	971.26	0.22	1904.03
2005-06	842.3	415.35	1443.06	0	27.00.71
2006-07	1224.93	516.15	1576.87	0	3317.95
2007-08	1513.87	518.74	1624.57	0	3657.28
Total	4925.28	2078.44	694.89	0.79	13953.40

Source: State Level Bankers Committee, BBSR.

During the period of study, the share of co-operative banks in financing to agricultural sector was 49.80 per cent followed by 35.30 per cent, 14.90% by RRBs and by OSFC respectively. The co-operative banks play a vital role in financing agricultural loans to farmers which covers 50 per cent total amount advanced. The table also shows that except the OSFC the other banks increases their finance to agriculture sector each year. In the year 2004-05 the cooperative banks financial target was Rs. 1443.06 cores which was higher by 67.31 per cent as composed to Rs. 971.26 cores financed in 2003-04. It is found that the performance of co-operative banks is quite satisfactory and maintain its priority in financing all the years. The situation of OSFC in financing is very insignificant which its only 0.79 per cent during past six years. In past three years from 2005-06 to 2007-08 OSFC has zero finance to agriculture farmers.

Table 8.2. Sectorwise target and achievement of banks in priority sector under the credit plan from 2002-03 to 2007-08

(in cores)

Year	*Agriculture*	*Industry*	*Service*	*Total*
2002-03				
Target	1303.49	282.43	893.10	2479.02
	(52.58)	(11.39)	(36.03)	(100)
Achievement	1046.57	145.62	1239.57	2431.76
	(43.04)	(05.99)	(50.97)	(100)
per cent of Achievement	80.29	51.56	138.79	98.09
2003-04				
Target	1393.65	289.79	1042.12	2725.55
	(51.13)	(10.63)	(38.24)	(100)
Achievement	1326.88	271.84	2951.85	4550.57
	(29.16)	(05.97)	(64.87)	(100)
per cent of Achievement	95.21	93.81	283.25	166.96
2004-05				
Target	1836.20	358.56	1315.06	3509.82
	(52.32)	(10.21)	(37.47)	(100)
Achievement	1904.03	252.06	2683.04	4839.13
	(39.33)	(5.23)	(55.44)	(100)
per cent of Achievement	103.69	70.30	204.02	137.87
2005-06				
Target	2513.43	1563.47	4415.42	
	(56.92)	(35.39)	(100)	
Achievement	2700.71	386.76	2566.54	55.94.01
	(48.28)	(6.91)	(44.89)	(100)
per cent of Achievement	107.45	113.91	160.42	126.69
2006-07				
Target	3199.50	486.10	2460.06	6145.66
	(52.06)	(07.91)	(40.03)	(100)
Achievement	3458.26	497.26	2784.23	6739.75
	(5131)	(738)	(41.31)	(100)
per cent of Achievement	108.09	102.30	113.18	119.67
2007-08				
Target	3738.57	775.54	2748.21	7262.32
	(51.48)	(10.68)	(31.84)	(100)
Achievement	642.21	2745.66	3657.28	7045.15
	(9.12)	(38.97)	(51.91)	(100)
5 of Achievement	82.81	99.91	97.83	97.01

Source: State Level Banker's Committee, Bhubaneswar

Sectorwise Credit

The District Level Coordination Committee (DLCC) of district prepares the Annual Credit Plan (ACP). As per the ACP, banks extend loan facilities to the priority sectors. Sectorwise target and achievement for all banks in Orissa in presented in Table 8.2.

Table 8.2 shows as the details of disbursement funds by banks to all the sectors in Orissa for the period 2002-03 to 2007-08. It can be observed from the above table that the total credit supply to agriculture sector increases every year from 2002-03 to 2007-08 Rs. 1046.57 crores to Rs. 3657.28 crores. During the year 2007-08 against the target Rs. 7262.32 crores was provided by bank as on 31,3,2008 under agriculture, industry and service sectors. The achievement was made 97.01 per cent of the target fixed out of the total amount invested Rs.7045.15 crores, agriculture sector received lion's share of 51.91 per cent followed by service sector (38.97 per cent) and industry sector only (9.12 per cent). The achievement under agriculture sector is more than the 100 per cent all the three years from 2004-05 to 2006-07 except 2007-08 it was 97.01 per cent only. During the year 2003-04 service sector received the lion's share of 64.87 per cent and agriculture sector 29.16 per cent where as 2007-08 agriculture sector received 51.99 per cent followed by service sector 38.97 per cent. Despite of erratic monsoon and prevalence of drought conditions in some part of the State, the performance of banks in crop loans segment of agriculture sector was quite satisfactory. The overall achievement of banks in agriculture sector has been boosted up. It has been targeted to invest Rs.8532.53 core during 2008-09 out of which Rs.4556.02 core has been fixed for agriculture sector, Rs.814.34 core for industry sector and Rs.3162.16 crores for service sector. It is observed that the performance of bank for financing agriculture sector in satisfactory and is improving in recent years.

Conclusions

Financial institutions play vital role in the development process of any country through supply of capital for production. The Indian banking system has undergone dynamic change during the post-nationalization period, *i.e.,* from 1969 and has emerged as one of the important institution for rapid economic growth. The vast network of financial institution helps the economy to augment its savings for more efficient utilizations. There has been a phenomenal growth and spread of banking services throughout the country particulars in rural areas.

It can be concluded from the study that all the financial institutions are showing satisfactory in financing to agriculture sector through out the study period. They always crossed the target fixed by Annual Credit Plan (ACP) in advancing credit to prints sector and the share of the credit to agriculture sector is quite significant. Advancing of credit by cooperative Bank to agriculture sector is highly satisfactory. Commercial Bank and RRBs are occupying on 2nd and 3rd position is financing to agriculture sector because their branches are rural oriented.

During the period 2002-03 to 2004-05 the share of service sector to total finance were 50.97 per cent, 64.87 and 55.44 per cent respectively, whereas during the period 2005-06 to 2007-08 the share of agriculture sector 48.28 per cent,51.31 per cent and 51.91 per cent respectively. During the six years study period, first three years (2002-03-2004-05) service sector dominant the more than 50 per cent share of total finance where as last three (2005-06 to 07-08) the agriculture sector occupy the major portion total finance.

REFERENCES

Economic Survey of Orissa.

Memoria, C.B and Dr. Berdri Bishal Tripthi (2007): *Agricultural Problems of India*, Kitab Mahal.

Vershney, P.N (2007) *Banking Law and Practice,* Sultan Chand and Sons.

9

Some Issues in Indian Agricultural Finance and New Actors in Financial Inclusion

S. Purushotham,[1]
D. Virajanand,[1]
P.L. Naidu[1]

Agricultural finance is the economic study of acquisition and use of capital in agriculture. It deals with the supply and demand for funds in the agricultural sector of the country. It includes direct and indirect finance. The credit can be obtained for different purposes from different sources under different terms and for different time periods.

On the basis of sources of borrowing, agricultural credit is broadly classified into institutional and non-institutional finance. Non-institutional or private sources include money-lenders, traders and commission agents, relatives and landlords; institutional sources consists of the government and co-operatives, commercial banks including the regional rural banks (RRBs).

The criteria for a good system of agricultural credit have been laid down by various economists. Tardy M. Louis presented some norms in his *Report on the system of agricultural credit and insurance* in 1938 to the League of Nations. Fredrick Nickolson framed a system in 1892. The All-India Rural Credit Survey Committee (1954 Gorwala Committee) and Reserve

[1] Lecturers in Deptt. of Economics, Government College (A), Rajahmundry.

Banke of India suggested some important features for the system of credit for modern agriculture.

From the above laid down norms it may be deduced that the availability of credit on adequate scale, on easy terms for sufficient length and time and repayability according to capacity constitute the important factors of a sound system of agricultural credit.

Credit is the most crucial ingredient in the agricultural production cycle. It has command over all other inputs required for production. Financing for agricultural development aims at the economic well being of the farmers in general and small and marginal farmers in particular. Credit can contribute to the improvement of net farm income in several ways.

The approaches adopted in institutional agricultural credit proved incapable of expanding to provide an appropriate volume and range of financial services. Many people believe that money lenders exploit rural households and the inexpensive formal credit enable farmers to escape from their evil grip.

A common thread found in agricultural studies is that developing institutional finance is one of the important policies for agricultural development. The institutional network for agricultural credit has grown substantially in quantitative terms but qualitatively not.

Functional structure of rural financial institutions is not conducive to meet financial services and needs of the agriculture and rural sector, i.e. they are mainly credit disbursing agencies. The rural financial institutions are non viable and have high transaction costs and hence a natural tendency on the part of banks to concentrate on small number of large farmers.

Rural financial institutions do not seem to consider financing of agriculture as a commercial proposition. They do not have a congenial recovery climate, hence higher proportion of Non Performing Assets on agricultural financing, Vast variations are seen in the flow of institutional credit. Moreover there is high risks rural lending. The share of commercial banks rural lending in total bank credit declining from over 16 per cent in 1990's to near 9 per cent in 2007.

Other than the above, there are certain other issues which are more relevant in India. The general tendency on the part of barrowers is to divert loan amount for consumption purposes and hence no substantial capital formation has taken place in the agricultural sector. Funds from the co-operative sector are diverted by the state governments to meet its financial requirements. Further the credit-deposit ratio is showing a declining trend.

The above mentioned issues in the area of agricultural credit have to be seen and require solutions. Stating from 1793, The Royal Commission on Agriculture gave a firm discussion on rural credit. The Magnacarta of India's rural credit we have *All-India Rural Credit Suvey Committee (Gorwala)*. In the later years there are like CRAFRICARD, NCA, Khusroo Committee reports maintained the tempo. Since 1990s there are reports on financial sector reforms and second one especially on agricultural credit.

Even after implementing so much in the area of institutional problems that are, a large number of poor continue to remain out side the fold of formal credit and banking system. Even after so much has been done by the Government, the RBI, and the NABARD in making the institutional credit frame work an inclusive one. But the result is not encouraging.

Despite having a vide network of rural bank branches in the country and the implementation of many credit linked poverty alleviation programs and innovative measures, the problem is still remains.

Practically all the institutions that are working in rural areas visa-vis Co-operatives Banks, RRB's and rural branches of Commercial banks are incurring losses. They are serving either with state subsidies or with cross subsidies. The problem of over dues constitutes one of the main issues of rural credit.

Keeping in view, these problems faced by institutional finance agencies, the Reserve Bank of India and NABARD, led to the evolution of self help groups and bank linkage model, as a cost effective and efficient mechanism for providing financial services to the unreached and underserved poor.

Besides SHG-bank linkage program, a number of NGO's had started experimenting the various initiatives like replication of Bangladesh's Grammena Bank's models, networking with NGO's and financing through SHG's federations and co-operatives to take the financial services to the poor.

The task force appointed by the NABARD with Nanda as its chairman defined micro-finance as "provision of thrift credit and other financial services and products of very small amounts to the poor in rural and semi urban areas for enabling them to raise their income levels and living standards" and financial institutions those which provide these are called Micro Financial Institutions (MFI's).

MFIs are under three Categories

1. Non-profit organizations registered as charitable institutions.
2. Mutual benefit MFIs such as state credit co-operative societies, National credit co-operatives and mutually aided co-operatives.
3. Non-banking financial companies - for profit MFIs.

Credit to rural and agricultural sector includes SHG-Bank linkage programme and lending by banks and financial institutions to MFIs for lending to ground level groups or individuals with the existing conventional or traditional lending program of banks. The task force made a strong case for formal recognition of MFIs just like institutional credit as a strategic tool for poverty alleviation and rural development and also suggested for a national policy on micro finance. Thus the agricultural credit system as developed and evolved over the years through reforms and policy initiatives are characterized by dualistic structures limited availability of collateral, covariant risks and seasonal fluctuations in the supply and demand for financial services as well as high transaction costs. There are different views on the co-existence of formal and informal suppliers of financial services in rural financial markets. The informal financial sector could be seen as an answer to the short comings of formal suppliers and extensive Government intervention. The elimination of these short comings would then lead to a gradual disappearance of the informal providers. The experience in the course of deregulation of the financial market has shown that informal financial sector is continuing to exist even in the presence of a growing formal financial market.

For a long-time rural financial markets were subject of massive government intervention. The problem situation was seen in a shortage of capital in rural areas, left of modern techniques in agriculture, limited saving capacity, and predominance of informal financial service providers as the source of funds. The subsidized state development banks, co-operatives, commercial banks, RRBs were not regarded as financial intermediaries but rather as mechanism to distribute funds which were to be impetus to productivity in agriculture. Today these approaches are considered as having failed largely.

The stress is for setting up of financially sustainable and widely outreaching financial institutions which fulfill an intermediary functions and in addition to demand oriented credit services also offer saving services. Formal as well as informal financial institutions are to be viewed on the basis of financial sustainability and outreach. In contrast to the earlier stereotype of inefficient exploitative money lenders, the range of informal financial service providers has now been agreed, analyzed and are accepted as important actors in rural financial market.

Since 87 per cent marginal farmers and landless laborers does not access credit from the formal system as noted by NCAER and World Bank in 2004. Non-institutional channels continue to have sway over micro-credit in India. Hence, Banks could be encouraged to undertake low cost wholesale lending to MFIs and through direct lending to low income clients.

Financial Inclusion

Micro-credit was being extended world over. The year 2005 was declared as the International Year of Micro-credit by the UNO. As per Reserve Bank of India, Financial Inclusion refers to delivering of banking services at an affordable cost to the vast sections of disadvantaged and low income groups who tend to be excluded from the formal banking channels.

A survey carried out and published in the Forbes website about Indian Micro-finance institutions and their positive ranking in the world for 2007 as many as seven leading MFIs have appeared in the list. The highest being Bandhan ranked at number 2.

Index of Financial Inclusion (IFI)

Mandira Sarma of ICRIER prepared and proposed first ever index of financial inclusion to find out the reach of banking service in 100 countries of the world. It is a multi-dimensional index with one single degit lying between 0 and 1 easy to compare across countries. India has been ranked 50th place above Russia and also below China.

Recommendations

Agricultural development is indispensable for economic growth. The major problem is with fulfilment of credit needs to the agriculture. For this

1. Enlisting of farmers clubs, SHG, NGOs and voluntary organizations.
2. Setting up of agricultural research stations.
3. Opening of vocational training centers for rural youth.
4. Stremeline and regulation of MFIs

Conclusion

Finally all the agencies involved should collaborate to work for development in order to achieve in eradication of poverty. Financial inclusion would result in reduction if not removal of poverty. Expert group on agricultural indebtedness recommended integration of MFIs with mainstream banking subject to the condition that these institutions moderate interest rates and abide by ethical banking practices.

10

Role of Institutional Credit for the Agricultural Development in India

Dr. Sudhansu Sekhar Nayak[1]

Introduction

Agricultural credit is considered as one of the most basic inputs for conducting all agricultural development programmes. In India there is an immense need for proper agricultural credit as Indian farmers are very poor. From the very beginning the prime source of agricultural credit in India was moneylenders. After independence, the Government adopted the institutional credit approach through various agencies like co-operatives, commercial banks, regional rural banks etc. to provide adequate credit to farmers at a cheaper rate of interest. Moreover, with growing modernisation of agriculture during post-green revolution period the requirement of agricultural credit has increased further in recent years.

Types of Agricultural Credit in India

Considering the period and purpose of the credit requirement of the farmers of the country, agricultural credit in India can be classified into three major types:

(*a*) **Short term credit :** The Indian farmers require credit to meet their short-term needs named *viz.*, purchasing seeds, fertilizers, paying wages to hired workers etc.

[1] Sr. Facualty, Dept. of Commerce, R.N. College, Dura, Berhampur, Orissa.

for a period of less than 15 months. Such loans; generally repaid after harvest.

(*b*) **Medium-term credit :** This type of credit includes credit requirement of farmers for medium ranging between 15 months and 5 years and it is required for purchasing cattle, pumping sets, agricultural implements etc. Medium-term credits are normally larger in size than short-term credit.

(*c*) **Long-term credit :** Farmers also require finance for a long period of more than 5 years just for the purpose of buying additional land or for making any permanent improvement on land like sinking of wells, reclamation of land, horticulture etc. Thus, the long term credit requires sufficient time for the repayment of such loan.

Sources of Agricultural Credit in India

In India agricultural credit is being advanced by different sources. The short-term and medium-term loan requirements of Indian farmers are mostly met by moneylenders, co-operative credit societies and Government. But the long-term loan requirements of the Indian farmers are also met by moneylenders, land development banks and the Government. Now-a-days the long-term and short-term credit needs of these institutions are also being met by National Bank for Agricultural and Rural Development (NABARD).

Sources of agricultural credit can be broadly classified into institutional and non-institutional sources. Non-Institutional sources include moneylenders, traders and commission agents, relatives and landlords, but institutional sources include co-operatives, commercial banks including the SBI Group, Reserve Bank of India and NABARD.

Non-Institutional Sources

Moneylenders

From the very beginning moneylenders have been advancing a major share of farm credit. Moneylenders are of two different types: (*a*) professional moneylenders (*b*) agriculturist moneylenders. These moneylenders were supplying a major portion of agricultural credit (69.7 per cent in 1951-52) and indulged into malpractice like manipulation of accounts and charged exorbitant rate of interest on their loan-often 24 per cent and over. Due to all these factors the share of moneylenders in total farm credit has declined sharply from 69.7 per cent in 1951-52 to 36.1 per cent in 1971 and then to only 16.1 per cent in 1981 and then to 7.0 per cent in 1995-96.

Traders and Commission agents

Traders and commission agents are also advancing loan to the agriculturist for productive purposes before the maturity of crops and then force the farmers to sell their crops at very low prices and charge heavy commission. This type of loans are mostly advanced for cash crops. The share of these traders in farm credit increased gradually from 5.5 per cent in 1951-52 to 8.8 per cent in 1961-62 and then sharply declined to 5.0 per cent in 1996. Thus its importance has been declining in recent years.

Relatives

Cultivators are also normally borrowing fund from their own relatives in times of their crisis both in terms of cash or kind. These loans are a kind of informal loans and carry no interest and are normally returned after harvest. The importance of this source of farm credit is also declining as its share of agricultural credit has already declined from 14.2 per cent in 1951-52 to 8.7 per cent in 1981 and then to 3.0 per cent in 1995-96.

Landlords

In India, small as well as marginal farmers and tenants are also taking loan from the landlords for meeting their financial requirements. This source has been following all the ill-practices followed by money-lenders, traders etc. Sometimes landless workers are even forced to work as a bonded labour. The share of this source to rural credit has increased from 3.3 per cent in 1951-52 to 14.5 per cent in 1961-62 and then sharply declined to 8.8 per cent in 1981 and then to 10.0 per cent in 1995-96.

Thus, the non-institutional sources of farm credit have been facing serious loopholes like exorbitant rate of interest, loan for unproductive purposes, non-repayment of loan etc.

Institutional Sources

The main motive of institutional credit is to assist the farmers in raising their agricultural productivity and maximising their income. Institutional credit is also not exploitative in character. The following are some of the important institutional sources of agricultural credit in India.

Co-operative Credit Societies

The cheapest and the best source of rural credit in India is definitely the co-operative finance. In India the active primary agricultural credit societies (PACS) cover nearly 86 per cent of the Indian villages and account for nearly 36 per cent of the total rural population of the country. The share of co-operatives in the total agricultural credit increased to nearly 40 per cent in 1996 as compared with only 3 per cent in 1951-52. In 1993-94 nearly 88,000 primary agricultural credit societies (PACS) of India provided Rs. 6461 crore as short term and medium term loans to the farmers.In 2004-2005. the same loan has increased to Rs. 30,639 crore, which was financed by co-operative banks.

Land Development Banks

Land Development Banks are advancing long term co-operative credit for 15-20 years to the farmers against the mortgage of their lands for its permanent improvement, purchasing agricultural implements and for repaying old debts. The number of State land Development Banks (SLDBs) increased from 5 in 1950-51 to 19 as on June 1986 which again consisted of 2447 Primary Land Development Banks (PLDBs) branches. The amount of loan sanctioned annually by these PLDB branches has increased from Rs. 3 crore in 1950-51 to Rs. 2039 crore in 1993-94. But benefits from these land development banks could not reach to small farmers and only the big landlords have been taking all advantages out of it. At present there are 19 central and 733 primary LDBs. In 1997, these banks advanced loan worth Rs. 1,744 crore.

Commercial Banks

In the initial period, the commercial banks of our country have played a marginal role in advancing rural credit. In 1950-51, only 1 per cent of the agricultural credit was advanced by the commercial banks. But after the nationalisation of commercial banks in 1969. the commercial banks started to extend financial support both directly and indirectly and also for both short and medium periods.

Regional Rural Banks

As per the recommendations of working Group on Rural Banks the Regional Rural Banks (RRBs) were established in. 1975 for supplementing the commercial banks and cooperatives in supplying rural credit. Since 1975 these Regional Rural Banks are advancing direct loans to small and marginal farmers, agricultural labourers and rural artisans etc for productive purposes. Till June 1996, in total 196 RRBs have been lending annually nearly Rs. 1500 crore to the rural people and more than 90 per cent of these loans were also advanced to the weaker section. At the end of 1988 these RRBs jointly advanced loan to the extent of Rs, 2,804 crore among 11 million persons lying below the poverty line. In 2004-2005, the RRBs have disbursed agricultural credit amounting to Rs. 11,718 crore which is just 10.17 per cent of total institutional credit to agriculture.

The Government

Another important source of agricultural credit is the Government of our country. These loans are known as taccavi loans and are lend by the Government during emergency or distress like famine, flood etc. The rate of interest charged against such loan is as low as 6 per cent. The share of the Government in the total agricultural credit has increased from 3.1 per cent in 1951-52 to 15.5 per cent in 1961-62 but then the share declined to only 5.0 per cent in 1996. During 1990-91, the state Governments had ADVANCED NEARLY Rs. 350 crore as short-term loan to agriculture. But the taccavi loan failed to become very much popular due to official red tapism and corruption.

Analysis

Table 10.1 shows the contribution of these different sources to the total agricultural credit in India since 1951-52 to 1996.

It can be revealed from Table 10.1 that among all the different non-institutional sources the contribution of moneylenders were highest and that was to the extent of 69.7 per cent. But its contribution gradually came down to 49.2 per cent in 1961-62 and then to 7.0 per cent in 1996. Total contribution of non-institutional source towards agricultural credit has gradually declined from 92.7 per cent in 1951-52 to 25.0 per cent in 1996. The share of institutional sources to the total agricultural credit which was 7.3 per cent in 1951-52 gradually increased to 18.7 per cent in 1961-62 and then to 75.0 per cent in 1996. Out of these institutional sources, co-operatives contributed 40 per cent and commercial banks contributed 30.0 per cent of the total farm credit in 1996.

Table 10.1. Borrowing of Cultivators from Different Sources (Percentages)

Sources	*1951-52*	*1961-62*	*1971*	*1981*	*1995-96*
A. Non-institutional					
(*i*) Moneylenders	69.7	49.2	36.1	16.1	7.0
(*ii*) Traders	5.5	8.8	8.4	3.2	5.0
(*iii*) Relatives and friends	14.2	8.8	13.1	8.7	3.0
(*iv*) Landlords and others	3.3	14.5	10.7	8.8	10.0
Total	92.7	81.3	68.3	36.8	25.0
B. Institutional					
(*v*) Government	3.1	15.5	7.1	3.9	5.0
(*vi*) Co-operatives	3.3	2.6	22.0	29.9	40.0
(*vii*) Commercial and Rural Banks	0.9	0.6	2.6	29.4	30.0
Total	7.3	18.7	31.7	63.2	75.0

Sources :

1. *All India Debt and Investment Survey, 1961-62.*
2. *All India Debt and Investment Survey, 1981*, Sarvekshana July, 1986.
3. *Economic Survey*, 1998-99.

Disbursement of Agricultural Credit in India in Recent Years

In recent years, the disbursement of agricultural credit has reached a new dimension. Co-operatives, commercial banks and Regional Rural Banks (RRBs) are advancing both short-term, medium term and long term credit to Indian farmers to help them to adopt modern technology and improved agricultural practices for raising crop productivity and production.

Table 10.2 shows the disbursement of agricultural credit by the institutional sources in recent years.

Table 10.2. Disbursement of Agricultural Credit since 1985-86

Item	*1985-86*	*1995-96*	*198-99*	*2000-01*	*2002-03*	*2004-05*
1. *Co-operative Banks*	2,787	8,331	12,571	16,564	20,247	N.A.
Short-term						
Mediu-term and Long-term	1,087	2,148	3,386	4,220	4,049	N.A.
Total	3,874	10,479	15,957	20,784	24,216	30,639
2. *Commercial and Regional Rural Banks*	3,131	11,553	20,903	31,930	46,514	84,604
Grand Total	7,005	22,032	36,860	52,714	70,810	1,15,243

Source : Economic Survey, 2005-2006. p. 165.

Table 10.2 reveals that total volume of agricultural credit has increased from Rs. 7,005 crore in 1985-86 to Rs. 10,186 crore in 1989-90 and then to Rs. 1,15,243 crore in 2004-2005. The target for 2005-2006 has been fixed at Rs. 1,41,000 crore. Moreover, among the various agencies disbursing agricultural credit, the amount of loan advanced by co-operatives has increased from Rs. 3,874 crore in 1985-86 to Rs. 10,479 crore in 1995-96 and then to Rs. 30,639 crore in 2004-05 but their share as percentage of total agricultural credit declined from 55.3 per cent to 47.5 per cent and then to 26.6 per cent respectively during (the same periods, he share of commercial banks and regional rural banks to the total agricultural credit has again increased from Rs. 3,131 crore in 1985-86 to Rs. 11,553 crore in 1995-96 and then to Rs. 84,604 crore in 2004-2005 and in percentage terms their share to total agricultural credit has also increased from 44.7 per cent to 52.4 per cent and then to 73. 4 per cent respectively during the same periods.

Again in 2004-05, the share of commercial banks alone in total institutional credit to agriculture is almost 63.2 per cent followed by co-operative banks with a share of 26.6 per cent. Regional rural banks account for just about 10.2 per cent of total credit disbursement. It is important to highlight the continued importance of short-term credit which accounts for two-third of the total institutional lending to agriculture.

Table 10.3 shows the flow of institutional credit to agriculture.

Table 10.3. Flow of Institutional Credit to Agriculture

(Rs. Crore)

Years	*Short Term*		*Medium and Long Term*	
	Amount	*Per cent*	*Amount*	*Per cent*
1993-94	11,271	68.4	5,223	31.6
1994-95	7,938	42.3	10,806	57.7
1995-96	14,526	65.9	7,507	34.1
1996-97	16,998	64.4	9,413	35.6
1997-98	20,640	64.6	11,316	35.4
1998-99	23,903	64.8	12,957	35.2
1999-2000	28,862	64.6	15,750	35.4
2000-2001	33,283	63.1	79,43!	36.9
2001-2002	40,961	64.0	23,039	36.0

Source : Economic Survey, 2002-03, p. 167.

Table 10.3 reveals that the flow of short-term institutional credit to agriculture which was Rs. 11,271 crore in 1993-94 gradually increased to Rs. 40,961 crore in 2001-02 and that of long-term institutional credit to agriculture has also increased from Rs. 5,223 crore in 1993-94 to Rs. 23,039 crore in 2001-02. In percentage terms, the flow of short-term institutional credit to agriculture which was 68.4 per cent in 1993-94 gradually declined to 64.0 per cent of the total credit in 2001-02 and that the share of long term credit has increased from 31.6 per cent in 1993-94 to 36.0 per cent in 2001-02.

Despite phenomenal increase in the volume of overall agricultural credit, there is a serious problem of over dues which has been inhibiting credit expansion on the one hand and economic viability of the lending institutions especially the cooperatives and the RRBs, on the other hand. The waiver of agricultural loans in 1990 has further aggravated the problem of recovery. In order to strengthen the co-operative credit structure of the country, the National Bank for Agricultural and Rural Development (NABARD) is contemplating an institutional strengthening programme. The Government has also introduced certain measures for revitalising the co-operatives on the recommendations of the Agricultural Credit Review Committee (1989). These measures include amendment to state co-operative laws, augmenting the reserve base of the Primary Agricultural Credit Societies (PACS), holding elections of co-operative bodies, revitalising PACS by business development planning and formulating Deposit Insurance Guarantee Scheme for PACS.

Measures

In order to improve the flow of credit to agriculture, the Government has introduced the following measures :

(1) Procedural simplificaiion for credit delivery has been made (as per R.V. Gupta Committee Report) through rationalisation of internal returns of banks.

(2) More powers have been delegated to branch managers to raise the credit flow to agriculture.

(3) Introduction of composite cash credit limit to farmers, introduction of new loan products with saving components, cash disbursement of loans, dispensation of no due certificate and discretion to banks on matters relating to margin security requirements for agricultural loans above Rs. 10,000.

(4) Introduction of at least one specialized agricultural bank

in each state to cater to the needs of high tech.

(5) Introduction of cash credit facility.

(6) Insuring Kisan Credit cards to farmers to draw cash for their production needs on the basis of the model scheme prepared by NABARD.

(7) The Government has made arrangement for hassle free settlement of disputed cases of over dues.

(8) To augment Rural Infrastructural Development Fund (RIDF) with a corpus of Rs. 10,000 crore with NABARD to finance rural infrastructure development projects by states.

Conclusion

From the above analysis it has been revealed that the extent of agricultural credit in India is very much inadequate and the private non-institutional sources still remained very important in supplying credit to the farmers. Further, the major problem of institutional credit faced by lending institutions, particularly the co-operatives, is the unsatisfactory huge level of overducs ranging between 40 to 47 per cent. This has resulted a bad health to the institutional credit and thus these lending institutions will not be able to advance more credit for meeting the growing needs of our farmers. Inspite of that, these institutional sources now-a-days are advancing more than 60 per cent of the required short term production credit of the Indian farmers. But the major portion of these credit is being appropriated by the 30 per cent of the middle and affluent fanners of India. At the end of the Seventh Plan, co-operatives, commercial Banks and RRBs extended credit facilities to the extent of Rs. 14000 crore as compared with only Rs. 24 crore in 1960-61.

REFERENCES

Conference volume, Indian Economic Association-2007, Kashmir.

Das and Mohapatra, *Indian Economy*, Kalyani Publishers, New Delhi, 08.

Dhingra, I.C., *'Rural Economics'*, Sultan Chand & Co, New Delhi, 1998.

District at a Glance, Goverment of Orissa, Bhubaneswar, 2008.

Dutt, Rudra and Sundaram K.P.M., *'Indian Economics'* Sultan Chand & Co, New Delhi, 2007.

Economic Survey, Government of Orissa, Bhubneswar, 2006-07 & 2007-08.

Kurukshetra, A journal on Rural Development, Vol. 56, No. 7 May, 2008.

Patnaik, B.Eswar Rao, "Problems and Prospects of Agricultural Development in Koraput District", Thesis un-published.

Stastitical Abstract of Orissa, Bhubaneswar, 2005 & 2008.

Yunus, Prof. Mohm. Grameen Bank, Micro Credit & Millennium Development-Goals, Economic & Political Weekly, Sept. 04-10-2004. Vol.XXXF/,N6.36.

11

Subsidies on Agricultureal Inputs and their Linkage to Consumer Benefits

Dr. P.V.S.N.G. Krishnam Raju[1]

Introduction

Government policies seek to strike a balance between agricultural and non-agricultural sectors of a country because they area interdependent. Everyone needs food to eat for living which is produced by the agricultural sector. Industries need raw materials such as sugarcane, cotton, coffee, tea, jute etc. produced by the agricultural sector without which they cannot run the industries. Other sectors such as tertiary sectors or service sectors also depend upon the agricultural sector for their business. These include the trading sector, the transport sector, the banking sector etc. This is called forward linkage. At the same time the agricultural sector is dependent on other sectors for its survival. The industrial sector provides fertilizers, machinery etc. to agriculture, transporters carry these products to the farmers fields, farmers, in turn, need many; non-agricultural products for their consumption. This is called backward linkage thus, there is a forward and backward linkage between the agricultural and other sectors in the country. Because of such a linkage, the happenings in the agricultural sector will have a great impact on other sectors of the country.

An increase in the prices of agricultural commodities (*i.e.*, food items) make the people spend more on their food

---

[1] Lecturer in Botany, Government College (A), Rajahmundry.

consumption and they will be left with less amount more on their food consumption and they are left with less amount of money to spend on other items. This is turn affects the demand for non-agricultural commodities and the industrial sector will suffer because of low demands. Similarly, an increase in the Prices of inputs used by agricultural sector pushes up the cost of production of agricultural commodities and the price of agricultural commodity itself will shoot-up. So there should be a balance between the happenings in the agricultural and non-agricultural sectors. The Government, through its various policies plays a major role in bring about such a balance. The present presentation focuses on; how one can derive the maximum benefit from the governmental price subsidies to agricultural inputs.

Cognition

A subsidy is that component of total money which a buyer need not pay to buy a commodity 9ie. Reduction in the cost of purchase subsidies are given usually to help the farmers buy better quality on inputs. Better quality of inputs, when used on the farms, helps to increase the production in the agricultural sector. Because a majority of our farmers are small farmers and poor it is estimated that about 72 of the farmers in India are small and marginal farmers. They cannot afford to buy good quality inputs at the market price. Their contribution to the production in agricultural sector is very important if the total production has to improve. If they keep on using the locally available resources seeds, manures etc., the product is low. The present improved technology in the agricultural sector is said to be capital intensive *i.e.* the formers need more money to adopt the improved technology. If the farmers do not use these improved inputs, the total agricultural production in the country will be low. Hence the Government (both state and central) provides a variety of subsidies to the agricultural inputs to encourage the farmers to use better quality of inputs on their farms. The type and quantity of subsidies given depend upon the needs which arise from time to time.

The subsidies given to the agricultural inputs come in different forms. The understand the nature of subsidies given to farmers we should know a brief history of what happened in midsities to cause green revolution in India in 1971-72.

The high yielding variety (HVV) programme was launched in Indian agriculture with the introduction of Mexican varieties of wheat in 1964-65. These varieties also acceptable to the Indians farmers. But the main disadvantage faced by the farmers at that time was that they had to buy these seeds from the market. Those varieties needed a higher use of chemical fertilizers and the formers did not have enough money with them to buy the inputs. Then the Government of India and many State Governments subsidized the farmers to buy HYVs and also chemical fertilizers. Later the schemes were extended to the high yielding varieties of rice and still latter to the other crops. The Government also made sure that sufficient funds were made available to the farmers as loans for which may major commercial banks were nationalized in 1969 and the banks were made to play a major role in financing the other cultural sectors. Thus the production of food grains in India reached a level of 100 million tones for the first time in 1971-723 that had resulted in green revolution in India. If the Government has not subsidized the input and not provided loans through banks green revolution could not have started in India.

TYPES OF SUBSIDIES

Subsidies on Seeds

Seed is the most important input for the growth of a crop. This is because what is produced depends upon the type of seed sown. The procedures for producing and distributing quality seeds is as follows.

Scientists in the research stations evolve good quality seeds after a series of trails on the research farms. These seeds which are released for multiplication are known as Breeder seeds. Breeder seeds are in turn multiplied (grown on a large scale) to produce Foundation seeds. Foundation seeds are then distributed to the farmers and private agencies for the purpose mass production of seed material. The production at the farmers level is closely watched for quality. The seeds which the farmers produce have to be certified by the certification agencies for their quality. The National Seeds Corporation and the State Seeds Corporation are the certifying agencies. Hence the seeds which can be used by the farmers for growing crops are known as certified seeds. The subsidy which comes into the picture in the case of seeds will mainly be at the breeders level. The research stations are run by the Government (Central and State) and the expenditure is almost entirely borne by the Government. If the farmers had to pay for running these institutions, then they would have to pay such high prices for seeds and that they certainly could not affords. Further, at the farmer's level, the price of certified seeds supplied by the seeds corporations through the Department of Agriculture is much less when compared to the same bought at open market prices from private traders. The Government spends a huge amount of money on running these organizations which not be transferred to the farmers. This amount forms a subsidy component on seeds.

Subsidies on Fertilizers

In India, the Government has pushed up the consumption of fertilizers by our farmers through its policies more than the farmers on their own. If the Government of India had not subsidized the fertilizer sector, our agricultural production would not have increased. Huge amounts of petroleum products are required for fertilizer production, which to a large extent have to be imported. Further, we also import huge qualities of fertilizers to fill the gap between demand and domestic production, thereby further pushing up the amount spent on acquiring fertilizers for our use. All these add up to a very high production bill on fertilizers.

The fertilizer factories have to be located at certain spots where there is a good supply of raw material. The fertilizers are then distributed to different consumption centers which are geographically scattered. The cost of transportation of fertilizers is high as they are bulky. The ensure uniformity in prices, the Government, through its agencies, has borne a large amount of the transportation costs which otherwise, would have to be paid by the farmers. Thus a major portion of fertisiers subsidies come in the form of absorption of import costs and transportation costs. It is estimated that the annual total subsidy on fertilizers is around Rs. 2000 crores.

Subsidies on Water (Irrigation) and Electricity

The subsidies on water and electricity are usually given by the State Governments. The water cess (tax) charged on the farmers to irrigate their fields are much lower than the water rated charged for other commercial purposes. In fact, major and medium irrigation projects are taken up by the governments to provide irrigation water to the farmers fields, These projects are treated as social utility projects and the costs are almost entirely met by the government. The water cess charged to the farmers for using this water is just enough to meet the maintenance cost for the projects. Hence, irrigation water in our country is highly subsidized. In the absence of such projects, our farmers fields would not get sufficient water for irrigation and they would have to depend upon rainfall. Rainfall being erratic, all our agricultural plans would be thrown out of great. Nearly 80 per cent of our five lakh villages are supplied with electricity. Farmers use electricity for their pump sets for drawing water to irrigate their fields. The charges on electricity used for irrigation purposes are much lower compared to the electricity charges levied on industries.

Subsidies on Agricultural Implements

Agricultural implements (like ploughs, seed-cum-fertiliser drills, etc.) are also subsidized by the State Governments. This is done to encourage the farmers to take up scientific methods of cultivation for getting better yields.

Subsidies on Agricultural Loans

Timely and adequate supply of credit is very important to the agricultural sector. Sowing, for example, is to be done during the first rains, or else the crop may fail. So, the farmer should have money to buy the seeds in time and carry our sowing operations. Hence, the Government has taken up a number of steps to ensure that the financial institutions (banks and Co-operatives) provide timely and adequate credit to the farmers.

In the case of agricultural credit, very poor farmers (small and marginal farmers) are entitled to subsidized loans. These come in the form of reduced interest rates to particular categories of farmers. Farmers belonging to back ward economic and social classes can get loans at lower rates of interest. The difference between the rate of interest charged to other farmers and that charged to the farmers in these classes forms the subsidy component

During times of distress like drought, floods, etc., it is observed that various State Governments either write off the loans borrowed by farmers (from the Co-operatives or banks) or waive off the interest chargeable on loans overdue. This facility is usually not enjoyed by the other sectors. This is done to protect the interest of the farmers during crisis and help them to continue in their agricultural operations. In the absence of such a measure many farmers will sell their loans and livestock at very low prices and migrate to the urban areas in search of a livelihood.

Mini-Kits

The latest development in the field of subsidies to the agricultural sector is providing 'mini-kits' to the farmers at the beginning of a cropping season. To encourage the farmers to use better quality of inputs, the Government through the Department of Agriculture, provide a package of inputs like seeds, fertilizers and other chemicals to the farmers in required quantities for scientific cultivation. These kits are either given free of cost to the farmers or they are charged very little. Similarly, such kits are given to the farmers to encourage production of important crops like pulses, oilseeds, etc.

Conclusion

The inputs used by the agricultural sector will be subsidized in many ways. The type of subsidy and the amount will depend upon the location of the farmer, (State, zone, etc.) crops grown, importance of the crop and the category to which the farmers belong. Other subsidies, such as regulated markets, all weather roads market information etc. are also given to the agricultural sector, though indirectly, which help the farmers.

The subsidies on inputs to agriculture reduce the prices the farmers pay to buy these inputs. Thus, the total cost of production of commodities becomes low. The price which the consumers buy their requirements depends on the cost of production to the producer and other factors. Consumer is also benefited by the subsidy polices of the Government to the agriculture sector.

Acknowledgements

I am thankful to the principal Capt. N.Ramakrishniah and the teaching faculty of the commerce department of Government College (A), Rajahmundry for their cooperation and encouragement to compile this presentation.

REFERENCE

Government Policies and Programmers - Economics of Food Vol II, IGNOU, School of Continuing Education.

12

The Micro-finance : Present and the Future Vision

Prof. R.N. Mishra,[1]
Mr. G. Chandayya,[2]

Micro-finance [Mf] traditionally defined by Marguerite S.Robinson[1]:

> "Microfinance refers to small scale financial services for both credits and deposits- that are provided to people who farm or fish or herd; operate small or microenterprise where goods are produced, recycled, repaired or traded; provided services; work for wages or commissions; gain income from renting out small amount of land, vehicles, draft animals, or machinery and tools; and to other individuals and local groups in developing countries in both rural and urban areas."

Since Independence, the Indian Government has made various efforts from encouraging expansion of the commercial bank branch network into rural and semi-urban areas, creation of local subsidiary banks known as regional rural banks [now it is called as a Andhra Pradesh Garmeen Vikas Banks in Andhra Pradesh] and promoting lending facilities to key disadvantaged economic sector. Despite much progress, the socio-economic impact has not been as strong as expected because commercial

---

[1] Professor, Department of Management Studies, Sanjay Memorial Institute of Technology, Berhampur

[2] Senior Faculty Member, Government Degree College, Rajahmundry (A.P.)

banks were not able to cater to this market in a cost-efficient and sustainable manner. Instead, bankers continued to view such lending as a social and more specifically, a regulatory obligation. Thus, financial organizations that were meant to serve the poor did not do the job to the extent originally planned.

Micro-finance has been in practice in India in one form or another since the 1970 and now widely accepted as an effective poverty alleviation strategy. The Indian micro-finance sector is a museum of several approaches found across the world. Indian micro-finance has lapped up the Grameen blueprint; it has replicated some aspects of the Indonesian and Bolivian. In India the movement commenced only in the 1990s due to the advent of financial sector reforms, which encouraged policy makers to devise and promote new solutions with a focus on repayment and sustainability. The movement started with the idea to connect a group of villagers, usually a group of 15-20 women, to commercial banks, which became widely known as the Self Help Groups [SHGs] Bank linkage model. In recent years, a new model of microfinance has emerged, which is closer to world famous Grameen model. This model involves financial intermediation by so called **"Micro-finance Institutions** [MFIs], which are specialized institutions created specifically to distribute credit to the un-banked populations.

Indian Micro-finance Institutions Approaches in Microfinance Sector

Indian Micro-finance institutions are following different models in micro-finance delivery based on their clients, focus area, interest rate, saving linkages, collateral, coverage and organizational structure. These models can be classified under Four Approaches namely:

1. SHGs/Group Promotion Approach
2. Micro Finance Institution Approaches
3. Micro Enterprise Development Approach and
4. Social Development Approach[2–3].

SHGs/Group Promotion Approach

It is based on the premise that NGOs or MFIs promote groups and provide those services of microfinance. This ultimately leads to build capacity of groups, in terms of savings mobilization, linking them with credit and providing technical support to the members of the group, for starting viable micro-enterprises.

Micro-finance Institution Approaches

It is based on the premise that Apex Financial Institutions [AFIs] provide bulk lending, soft loan and some grants to such NGOs can act as MFIs and on lend to the poor people, SHGs, Federations and Similar NGOs. These MFIs stimulate credit demand of the needed people. They also provide technical support to the beneficiaries to ensure proper utilization of loan and repayment. At the same time, they meet their cost of funds, cost of credit management and cost of default, through the spread of interest and generate surplus for the viable operation of microfinance.

Micro Enterprise Development Approach

This refers to the package of services, policies, programmes and institutions, intended to develop micro-enterprises including lending and savings. Micro-finance sector is providing help to solve the problem of credit for developing micro-enterprises. Thus, micro-finance for micro-enterprises development has emerged as important approach in India.

Social Development Approach

It is based on the premise that people should earn money by investing in viable micro-enterprises. They should earn profit from their enterprises. Major share of the profit should be reinvested in enterprises for their growth. The other share of the profit should be spent on social development i.e. health, education, housing, sanitation and nutrition food etc. By earning profit from the viable micro-enterprises, people will increase their paying ability for services delivered to them under different social development projects run by NGOs and Governments.

The Role of Apex Financial Institutions [AFIs] has been very significant, since the emergence of microfinance sector all over world. In the case India, it is true - National Bank for Agriculture and Rural Development [NABARD], Small Industries Development Bank of India [SIDBI], Rashtriya Mahila Kosh [RMK], National and International Financial Institutions have made their entry in this sector by providing loans and grants to NGOs/MFIs for different income generating projects. Through Mf has proved important development intervention for Poverty alleviation, Empowerment and Employment generation in India as well as anywhere in poverty driven countries in the world. But the major issue in Mf intervention is of its financial sustainability. Most of the Mf Progrmmes so far are not cost-effective and depended on grants and donations to recover their high cost operations as well as other costs involved in micro-financing. As a result of it, interest's rates are very high in Mf Programmes at par with market rates of interest of financial isnstitutions. The other major issue in Mf intervention is of its scaling up. Given the magnitude and extent of poverty in India, there is a need to expand Mf services at a fast rate. However, problem of sustainability in operation becomes hindrance for scaling up Mf services.

Indian Bankers Practices in Microfinance

In India, National Bank for Agriculture and Rural Development [NABARD] launched an experimental pilot project in February 1992 with Mysore-based Non-Government Organizations [NGO]-MYRADA in Karnataka by promoting Self-Help Groups [SHGs]. Self-Help Groups have been recognized by the policy makers as the effective channels for accomplishing the distributional objectives of monetary policy. Group model as developed by Bangladesh Grameen Bank is by and large followed in most of the south Asian countries. In this pilot project, the strategy involved forming small, cohesive and participative groups of the poor, encouraging them to pool their thrift regularly and using the pooled thrift to make small interest bearing loans to members and in the process learning the nuances of financial discipline[4]. Subsequently, bank credit also becomes available to the group, to augment its resources for lending to its members.

It may be emphasized that NABARD sees the promotion and banking linking of SHGs not as a credit programme but as a part of an overall arrangement for providing financial services to the poor in a sustainable manner and also an empowerment process for the women members of these SHGs. In this pilot project the Reserve Bank of India financial supported, it aimed at promoting and financing 500 SHGs across the entire country.

The SHGs-Bank linkage strategy has now come a long way. The strategy involves financing of SHGs promotion of SHGs promoted by external facilitators like NGOs, bankers, socially spirited individuals and Government Agencies, as also promotion of SHGs by themselves and financing SHGs directly by bank or indirectly where NGOs and similar organizations act as financial intermediaries as well. Through the self-help bank linkage programme the RBI and NABARD sought to improve relations existing between the poor and bankers with social intermediation of NGOs[5].

Later on, Small Industries Development Bank of India [SIDBI] also came forward to provide bulk lending to NGOs for on lending to groups/individuals. Ministry of Human Resource Development, Government of India established Rashtriya Mahila Kosh [RMK] for providing loan to NGOs to on lend to poor women SHGs. Other National and State financial Corporations also enter into the Microfinance Sector. Besides this, the International funding agencies *i.e.* CARE-INDIA, PLAN International, World Vision, PLAN NET etc. also started Microfinance services in India through their projects.

The Future Vision For Micro-finance

With an estimated untapped market of nearly a billion poor people, microfinance now stands at a crucial crossroad. Successful microfinance NGOs have proved that financial services can be an effective and powerful instrument for poverty reduction by enhancing the ability of poor people to increase Incomes, build assets, and reduce their vulnerability in times of economic stress. There is greater consensus than ever before about what is needed to make microfinance sustainable. Yet with most poor people still lacking access to basic financial services, microfinance has yet to reach its full potential.

Over the next decade, microfinance will either realize its vast potential for improving the lives of large numbers of the poor - or it will remain an unfulfilled promise. Much depends on the extent to which the international development and financial communities can partner with social entrepreneurs and governments in developing countries to develop financial systems for the poor that are far broader than those that currently exist. Of course, macroeconomic policies and individual sector improvements will need to underpin the development of such financial systems: finance alone is clearly not enough.

This new vision is a world in which diverse poor people enjoy permanent access to a wide range of financial services, delivered through a variety of convenient mechanisms by different types of institutions. The concept of financial services to the poor will no longer be dominated by micro-credit, but will recognize the importance of such other services as savings, payment services, and insurance. Providers will include not only non-governmental microfinance Institutions (MFIs), but also savings and credit cooperatives, commercial banks, community finance institutions, consumer credit companies, insurance companies, and other financial Institutions.

Increasing competition among products and institutions will result in greater efficiency, benefiting both financial institutions and clients. Advances in technology will lead to reduce transaction cost, enabling volumes to grow and marginal costs to decline. New technologies will also improve client information and asset and liability management, reducing risk and thus costs. In this vision, national policymakers understand that financial systems can and should work for all levels of society, especially for the poor who constitute the overwhelming majority of their populations.

This vision embraces institutions that are motivated to provide sustainable financial services to the poor because it makes economic sense, as well as those driven by the objectives of poverty alleviation and/or job creation. Encouraging a more diverse range of organizations with different objectives, and different needs for subsidy, will enable outreach to a broader range of poor clients, from growing urban micro enterprises to very poor rural households.

This transformation of perspective is urgent, as the growth of poverty and unrealized human potential outpaces the incremental growth of microfinance. This transformation is also within our reach because many of the necessary elements needed to scale up microfinance are already in place. Banks and other institutions with nationwide distribution systems are beginning to take interest in reaching poorer clients. A great deal of the knowledge about the requirements of sustainable microfinance already exists. Advances in information technology have never been so promising to lower the cost and risk of delivery mechanisms. The challenge before us is to mobilize this knowledge and apply it on a much vaster scale. Before tackling this enormous challenge, however, it is important to address the basic/question of what microfinance is, why it is important, and how it contributes to development.

What is Micro-finance in Present Scenarios?

As recently as a few years ago, the term "micro-finance" was easily understood: a credit methodology that employs effective collateral substitutes to deliver and recover short-term, working capital loans to micro entrepreneurs (or potential micro entrepreneurs). The vision was that micro enterprises of clients would grow, increasing their incomes and sometimes creating employment, lifting the poor out of poverty. The promise of sustainability meant that microfinance could leverage relatively scarce donor funding by attracting much larger pools of private capital, thus expanding outreach to massive numbers of the poor. The non-governmental organizations (NGO's) that pioneered this methodology and have provided most of the micro loans to date would grow, become independent from donors, and possibly transform into banks for the poor, without losing their social mission.

Today the picture has become far less clean, the storyline more nuanced, and the boundary between microfinance and other financial services blurred. We recognize that the micro-finance world as it has been narrowly defined is but a small segment of the universe of financial services to poor people. Traditional microfinance has encountered several core challenges to a number of its basic premises :

- Not all the poor run growing micro enterprises, but all poor people need, use, and benefit from different kinds of financial services. In fact, poor people are extremely diverse and their needs vary widely with their circumstances.
- Supply-driven credit methodologies have reached a relatively narrow band of potential clients within the spectrum of the poor, often leaving behind both extremely poor and remote clients, and the less-poor with larger enterprises.
- The types of financial services needed by poor people extend far beyond working capital loans, encompassing an array of savings, credit, insurance, and money transfer services. Convenient, safe and secure deposit services are a particularly crucial need.
- NGO's, while crucial for experimenting with new models and conducting research and development, face challenges in governance, legal frameworks, and cost structures. More importantly, they generally have not reached massive scale or independence from donors (although there are major exceptions to this rule).
- While they are few, several successful microfinance NGO's have demonstrated that it V is possible to achieve financial self-sustainability while reaching the very poor with extremely small loan sizes, even the very poor in sparsely populated areas.
- Institutions with large existing infrastructures, such as commercial and state-owned banks, credit union networks, financial cooperatives, and even retail chains, may offer a significant, if challenging, "Answer" to the problem of scaling up financial services for the poor.
- These lessons learned point to an expanded view of our task: microfinance is about diverse institutions providing massive, permanent access to a broad range of financial services for a broad range of clients.

The Role of Microfinance in Reducing Poverty

At the core of microfinance is a fundamental belief that access to financial services protects and empowers the poor by mitigating them from risks and giving them choices. Financial services help the poor cope with a common feature of their lives: vulnerability. Whatever they save or borrow, evidence shows that when poor people have access to financial services in the absence of emergency conditions, they choose to invest their savings or loans in a wide range of assets. These "assets" can be sending children to school, buying better medicines and more nutritious food, fixing a leaky roof, meeting social and cultural obligations like paying for and funerals, as well as building income-generating potential by investing their enterprises.

The multiple roles of financial services for the poor parallel the multiple dimensions of poverty captured in the Millennium Development Goals (MDGs). The MDGs have galvanized the development community around measurable and concrete indicators of poverty reduction. Financial services put power into the hands of the poor to pursue their own strategies for building human, physical, economic and social capital to escape poverty. And because microfinance services can be delivered sustainably within relatively short periods of time, benefits can be delivered on a permanent basis, well beyond the duration of donor or government programs that rely on continuous subsidies. Far from being a narrowly defined, specialized field occupying a small corner of development thinking and practice, micro-finance is an important foundation for poverty alleviation and the wider development agenda. It supports other development efforts and can make a significant difference in the way of poor people address those development problems on their own terms.

How does Microfinance Contribute to the Millennium Development Goals (MDG'S?)

A review of microfinance literature points to several specific conclusions about the impact of microfinance

On Poverty Reduction and Several other MDGs

- **Eradicate Extreme Poverty and Hunger :** Extensive evidence demonstrates that microfinance helps reduce poverty through increases in income, allowing the poor to build assets and reduce their vulnerability.

- **Achieve Universal Education :** Households that have access to microfinance spend more on education than non-client households. Improvements in school attendance and the provision of educational materials are widely reported in microfinance households. Participation in credit and savings programs has enabled many families to send several children at a time to school, and has reduced drop-out rates in higher primary grades.
- **Promote gender equality and women's empowerment :** Microfinance clients are overwhelmingly female. Micro-finance has been widely credited for empowering women by increasing their contribution to household income, the value of their assets, and control over decisions that affect their lives.
- **Reduce child mortality, improve maternal health, and combat disease :** Microfinance contributes to improved nutrition, housing, and health, especially among women clients.

Micro-finance and Financial Sector Deepening

Until now, microfinance has largely developed outside the realm of the formal financial sector on a separate track that seldom interacts with established financial actors. When governments and donors address financial sector issues, broad concerns such as banking sector reform, capital market development, and corporate governance are generally at the top of their agenda, not microfinance. For its part, the microfinance community of practitioners, donors, and technical experts has argued, perhaps too convincingly, in favor of microfinance as a highly specialized sector that needs separate standards techniques and/or legal frameworks to be effective.

These arguments made sense at the time when the need to professionalize microfinance into a more business-like activity became apparent. However, the efforts to make microfinance something separate have also served to isolate it as a marginal sector disconnected from the broader financial system.

It is becoming increasingly apparent that large-scale sustainable microfinance can be achieved only if financial services for the poor are integrated into the overall financial system. This means that microfinance, or financial services for the poor, becomes the lower end of the entire financial sector, opening up access and markets to increasingly poor and geographically remote clients. It means achieving financial sustainability not through high interest rates alone, but by leveraging technology and streamlining business processes to increase cost efficiency in the face of competition. If means attracting new players and new sources of commercial and quasi-commercial debt and equity capital. It means promoting transparency that allows the outside world to understand and judge the performance of micro-finance *vis-a-vis* other financial and non financial services and other development interventions. It means governmental policies that promote financial sector deepening and expansion. It means seeing microfinance as greater than microcredit and micro-enterprises - as financial services for the poor. It also means ensuring that the social values-driven mission of micro-finance is not unintentionally compromised as a result of this integration. The "financial systems approach" to micro-finance has generally meant a focus on one dimension of this vision - the sustainability and formalization of micro-finance institutions. True, the paucity of strong retail institutions remains the principal bottleneck to meeting the massive demand for financial services among the poor. However, just as there is wide diversity in poor clients and their needs and circumstances, so must there be a wide range of service providers motivated by varied objectives. This vision upholds the essential principles of financial sustainability in order to allow for growth, and it calls for acknowledgement and clarification of the role of subsidies in institution and support organizations that are doing work that merits subsidy.

Current Actors in the Microfinance System

Over the Past 30 years, the micro-finance industry has grown to encompass many types of actors with different objectives, roles, and comparative advantages. Clearly, no single organization has the means or the capacity to achieve the expanded vision of microfinance on its own. Developing financial systems that work for the poor will require improved dialogue, coordination, and partnership among these different actors, as well as building better linkages with other development sectors.

Providers of financial services to the poor

Micro-finance suppliers can be divided into three broad categories: (*i*) traditional and informal providers, such as moneylenders, pawn shops, and rotating savings and credit associations (ROSCAs); (*ii*) formal unlicensed institutions such as microfinance NGO's; and (*iii*) licensed financial intermediaries, including commercial and state-owned banks, credit unions, community finance institutions, consumer credit companies, and finance companies. Understanding will reveal where the gaps are and what can be done to meet the needs of those who are not being served.

Networks

Intermediary organizations have, and will continue, to play a critical role in microfinance. Such organizations include national associations of microfinance institutions, regional or global networks of MFIs or credit unions, and even some investment funds that provide governance and technical assistance to MFIs. Networks serve several crucial functions in expanding the delivery of financial services to the poor. First, they are an important voice in policy and regulatory change, both within countries and across regions. Second, they can be an effective means of intermediating ground. Third, they are potent force for improving the performance of their members through peer learning, information exchange, and mutual accountability. Fourth, networks that provide funding to members, such as through investment funds, sometimes fulfil a governance function that is more effective and closer to true commercial governance than what donors provide.

Donors

Virtually all donors, including private, local, bilateral, and multilateral donors, as well as local and international NGOs, support micro-finance activities in some way: through grants, subsidized loans, guarantees, or technical assistance. The approach of donors - and the requirements they set for microfinance institutions to access their funds can significantly after the development of the sector. Even as some financial service institutions "graduate" to commercial funding, there will always be a role for donors to subsidize development work that is not commercially viable, either because of the risk or the cost. Donor subsidies, for example, can motivate new financial institutions to enter the market by defraying development and technical assistance costs. The role of subsidies in microfinance is important, but need to be more clearly defined, as does the role of donors' *vis-a-vis* other, more commercial funding sources.

Private Investors

There is widespread recognition that in order to reach scale, microfinance needs to move from dependence on donor funding to reliance on more abundant commercial funding and domestic savings. Most private capital that supports micro-finance takes the form of institutional deposits attracted by licensed institutions. While private capital still represents only a small fraction of total funding, a range of private flinders/investors - from commercial banks to socially responsible investors - are becoming increasingly interested in microfinance as more microfinance institutions demonstrate the profitability of banking for the pocr. An important requirement for attracting greater private resources into microfinance is reliable information on the performance of financial institutions serving the poor. Another important requirement is mechanisms that can better match the demand for funds on the part of well-performing or high-potential institutions with the supply of available funds.

Governments

Depending on their approach, governments can either undermine or encourage the development of micro-finance. In general, the government's role in microfinance should be to maintain or create an enabling environment that permits the growth of financial services for the poor and the integration of the poor in the broader economy. Governments can do this by addressing broad legal and regulatory constraints -such as cumbersome business registration procedures, corruption, or inflexible property rights laws - which, while not specific to the poor, may place an undue burden on them. An important element of this strategy is a regulatory framework that allows a wide array of financial intermediaries to serve the poor. Interest rate ceilings have to be relaxed or remove so that micro lenders can cover their costs. Licensing rules need to.be adjusted so that financially solid institutions can fund their lending activities with deposits from the public. Governments should get out of the business of directly providing financial services to the poor, eliminating subsidized and inefficient lending programs that foster a culture of non-repayment on the part of clients and undermine goods microfinance institutions. Depending on the size of the microfinance sector, special attention should be paid to building the capacity of bank regulators to evaluate, monitor, and supervise microfinance institutions in a way that ensures the overall soundness of the sector without stilling its growth.

Technical Service Providers

As microfinance has evolved, a private industry of service providers to support microfinance institutions has come into being. This service industry encompasses technical advisers, audit firms, credit bureaus, rating agencies, trainers or training institutes, technology and information systems specialists. The lack of local capacity to provide these services has resulted in over reliance on international expertise and thus high costs of these services. Building both the market for these services and the local human resources base to meet market demand is a key condition for the development of a sustainable microfinance industry.

NOTES

1. Marguerite S. Robinson, "Microfinanance: the paradigm shift from credit delivery to sustainable financial Intermediation", in Mwangi S Kimenyi. RobertC Wieland and JD Von Pischke [Eds] 1998, *Strategic Issues in Microfinance,* Ashgate Publishing: Alder shot.
2. Singh, Naresh [2002] "Perspectives on Emergence and Growth of Microfinance Sector", Discussion Paper No. 13 Mumbai: Narsee Monjee Institute of Management Studies.

3. Singh, Naresh [2004]" A comparative study of Approaches of Micro finance Delivery Systems in Bangladesh and India", Discussion Paper No.22 Mumbai: Narsee Monjee Institute of Management Studies.

4. Mohanan'S [2000] Micro Credit and Empowerment of women-Role of NGOs, *Yojana*, 44 (2) : 22-28.

5. Bansal, H [2003] SHG-Bank linkage programme in India: an overview', *Journal of Micro-finance* 5: 21-49.

6. Extracted from CGAP Phase III Strategy Paper 2003-2004.

13

Regional Rural Banks and Self-help Groups: Harbingers of Development

Dr. B. Eswar Rao Patnaik,[1]
Mr. Rajesh Pashu Palak[2]

In recent years, Self-help Groups have emerged as the real grass root setups for micro-credit growth and rural development in countries, such as Bangladesh, Sri Lanka, Malaysia, Pakistan and India. The genesis of Grammen banks in the world economy may be traced to the birth of Grammen bank in Bangladesh in 1975-76, when the noble laureaute Prof. Muhammad started lending $27 to 42 people in a village (Jobra) near Chittagong University, where he was teaching. To quote pro. Yunus "while providing small loans to poor is an economic intervention, it begins a process of transformation in the life of an individual member. A woman who believe she has no worth starts to believe in her ability to improve her own life". R.R.Bs have a pivotal role to play in accelerating the pace of rural development in India in general and in Orissa in particular, where over 40per cent of people do not have bank accounts as per the N.S.S 59th round. Twenty-seven per cent of farmers of the country received credit from formal sources and 22 per cent from informal sources. The remaining 51per cent mostly marginal farmers have virtually no access to credit. Despite five and half decades of plan exercise in India' a vast segment of population live below poverty line. A question emerges : 'have Grammen Banks succeeded in serving as a small man's Bank?'.

[1] Reader in Economics, SBRG Womens College, Berhampur.
[2] Jr. Lecturer (Economics), R.N. College, Dura, Berhampur.

The present study makes an effort to analyze dispassionately the role of RRBs in accelerating the development self-help groups. The exercise has concentrated on the performance of RRBs in India and Orissa province. The study is primarily based on secondary data assembled from plan documents of government of Orissa, standard texts, dailies like, *New Indian express* and *E.P.W.*

GOALS AND PERFORMANCE OF RRBs

It is well-known that, credit is a vital input in the process of development and an accelerator of development. Five Grammen Banks have initially commenced their operations in Mordabad and Gorakpur in Uttar Pradesh, Biwani in Harayana, Jaipur in Rajasthan and Malada in West Bengal. The principal objectives of Regional Rural Banks (RRBs) in India were to (lend) serve agriculture, trade and allied activities, to achieve an inclusive growth rate in GDP, to implement poverty eradication programmes, like, I.R.D.P and Sampoorna Grammen Swarojagar Yojana, inculcate thrift and savings in the minds of people, open new branches in growth potential areas and ameliorate the socio-economic conditions of women by financing women self-help groups. The area of operation of RRBs is limited to one or two districts and RRBs cover small and marginal farmers, landless labour, the artisan and the resource-poor. The focus of RRBs is on handicapped persons through financing them in self-employment schemes and provision of loan for securing artificial limbs.

Performance of RRBs

An evaluation study of RRBs by Reserve Bank of India (1981) has revealed that, Grammen Banks have accelerated the development of agriculture by provision of loans to farmers for crop production, irrigation, equipments and implements, and for land development. RRBs have succeeded in catering to the finance required by primary agricultural credit societies and farmers societies. They are cheap and viable alternative to exploitative money-lenders and they enable cultivators to find an escape from the clutches of shylok like money-lenders.

It is heartening to note that, the aggregate deposits of RRBs numbering to 196 at country level stood at Rs. 43,220 crore in 2007-08 and advances disbursed by them were as high as Rs. 1,83,720 crores in 2007-08. The Narasimhan Committee has appreciated the role of RRBs in providing access to the economically weaker sections of society. One feather to the cap of success of RRBs is the net profits made by them, that touched Rs. 790 crore in 2001.

It follows that, branch expansion and credit growth have reached at an appreciable level in the post-nationalization period. Access to institutional credit by rural poor has improved to a great extent. However, 80per cent of rural poor are indebted to informal sources in cash or kind. Of late, intervention has come forth from people themselves in form of self-help groups.

SELF-HELP GROUPS

The growth of self-help groups as powerful tool for empowering women at country level is the result of NABARD's work (pilot project) for promoting 500 self-help groups in India. Following the success of the project, the Reserve Bank of India has issued directives to banks in 1996 to cover SHGs as a mainstream activity under priority sector lending portfolio.

The self-help group is a small economically homogeneous and affinity groups of rural poor not exceeding 20 members, voluntarily coming together to save small amounts regularly to mutually agree to contribute to a common fund, to have collective decision-making to resolve conflicts through, collective leadership and mutual discussions, and provide collateral free loans at terms decided by members at market driven rates (Revati, 2007). The following are the cardinal features of SHGS.

Features of SHGs

SHGs generate a common fund for which each member contributes his savings on a general basis.

- The group conducts regular meetings once in a week. The meeting involves collection of savings by members and lends funds to needy members for productions and consumption purpose.

- The meeting decides borrowers by consensus.
- Small amounts of loan carrying low rates of interest are provided to members.
- Loan procedure is simple and flexible.
- SHGs borrow from banks or voluntary agencies to lend to members.
- NGOS may help SHGs in procuring raw materials and marketing of the produce.
- They elect among them a leader and sub-leader to manage group and activities.

The SHG model is a financial delivery model which has its objectives of reaching to the unreached poor in a cost effective manner with the help of participating financial institutions. The three major actors in rural development are :

(1) The SHGs,

(2) The Banks as suppliers of credit, and

(3) NGOS, Government agencies and individuals.

MICRO-FINANCE, RRBs AND SHGs

The total number of SHGs covered by RGBs at country level has increased from 230 in 1998-99 to 8,271 in 2005-06 (RGB annual report 2006). There has been a steep increase in the number of women members covered under SHG assistance by RGB from 207 in 1998-99 to 1,14,550. The Outlay of RGB has picked up from Rs. 20.03 lakhs in 1998-99 to Rs. 24.17 core in 2005-06.

Features of Micro-finance

(*a*) Micro-finance to Prof. Yunus refers to these kinds of collateral free loans for income generating activities of people.

(*b*) It promotes credit as a human right.

(*c*) Its mission is to help poor people to help themselves to overcome poverty.

(*d*) It is offered for creating self-employment for income generating activities.

Table 13.1. Number of SHGs linked Banks as on 31st March, 2006

Sl.	Banks	2004		2005		2006	
		No of SHGs	Credit Rs.	No of SHGs	Credit (Rs)	No. of SHGs	Credit Rs.
1.	Commercial	5,38,422 50%	22,548.322 58%	8,43,473(52%)	1,18,807	69877.0(61%) (53%)	
2.	RRBs	405,998 (38%)	12,782.5 (33%)	563,842(35%)	20,995.5(31%)	740.024 (32%)	38,22115(29%)
3.	Cooperatives	1,34671 (12%)	3711.2(9%)	211,137(13%)	6398.9(9%)	310,194 (14%)	1,08771,8(10%)
4.	Other	00	00	00	00	271	5.2%
	Total	10,79091 (100%)	39,042.0 (100%)	16,18456(100%)	6894.6(100%)	2238565 (100%)	113,975.5 (100%)

Source : Kurukshetra Volume 55, (12) October 2007. pp. 11.

(*e*) It is initiated as a challenge to conventional banking which rejected poor as non-credit worthy.

(*f*) It requires borrowers to join in groups to obtain loans. Loans are received in a continuous sequence, with new loans becoming available as previous loans are recovered.

(*g*) It comes with both obligations and voluntary programmes from borrowers.

Table 13.1 depicts that as on 31st March, 2006 number of SHGs linked with banks were 22,38,565 a compared to 10,79,091 in 2004. The share of commercial banks in respect of number of SHGs linked with banks and credit was the highest followed by RRBs and cooperatives.

The SHG movement has added a significant dimension to micro-finance system in the country. There is uneven spread of SHG movement in the country. Bulk of its activities are concentrated in India *i.e.,* Andhra Pradesh, Tamil Nadu, Karnataka and Uttar Pradesh. A vast segment of population subject to material deprivation, intellectual deprivation and social deprivation do not come under the purview of SHGs.

The Reserve Banke of India has advised the banks to adopt SHG financing as main business and provide credit support. NABARD has been playing the anchor role in popularizing by creating awareness among bankers through seminars/workshops organizing training programmes for bankers, NGOs, grass root SHGs and provides refinance @100per cent to banks on their advances to SHGs and on a selective basis grant on reimbursement basis, the administrative cost of NGOs.

The initiative by NABARD in involving CENDERT in KBK district for boosting SHG credit linkage programme will produce good results in 2001-2002. NABRD's initiatives to involve bankers in promotion of SHGs by way of selecting and designating 5 branches as Self-help Promoting institutions has started bearing results inasmuch as about 80SHGs have been promoted by them. NABARD has also started sanctioning promotional grant to NGOs for promoting SHGs. So far two such proposals to NGOs namely Sarbodaya Samiti, Koraput and CYSD, Boipariguda have been sanctioned.

Table 13.2.

Name of the branch	*No. of SHGs linked*	*Promoter*
KPGB, Jeypore	6	ILDP
KPGB, Kundra	4	CYSD
KPGB, Ramgri	8	CYSD
KPGB, Ambaguda	6	ILDP
KPGB, Phampuni	1	ILDP
KPGB, Chalanguda	3	Agril.Dept. Bank and Block
KPGB, Sosahandi	4	-do-
KPGB, Pottangi	7	-do-
KPGB, Lamtaput	7	Jaguri
KPGB, Kakiriguma	5	WORD
KPRGB, Padwa	6	RASS
KPGB, Jolaput	4	SPREAD
KPGB, Padwa Lamp	8	RASS
KPGB, Laxmipur	10	SAMFA
KPGB, Jeypore	1	ILDP
Union Bank, Jeyopre	1	ILDP
Total	81	

The brief profile of micro-finance for Koarput is presented below :

Total number of blocks in the district	14
Number of blocks where SHGs exist	14
Total number where SHGs are credit linked	11
No. of NGO sin the district	About 200 NGOs of which 20 are active

The SHG linkage has started taking root in the district though on a small scale. The feather to the cap of success of

Koraput Panchavati Gramya Bank is the provision of credit assistance to eight groups promoted by Ankurarn in Narayanapatna block in 1994-95. In 1996-97 KPGB provided assistance to five groups.

The Arithmetics of Table 13.2 suggest that, KPGB has provided credit in Jeypore, Kundra, Ramgiri, Ambaguda, Phampuri Chalanguda, sosahundi, Pottangi, Lamtapt Kakkirigumma, Jalaput blocks of Koraput district. Out of 14 blocks of the district 11 Blocks are credit linked Table 13.2.

Case Study 1

Smt. Padma Hontal W/o Shadeb Hontal of village Bondakatra was used to cultivate Niger. She had an annual income of Rs. 2,000 in 1996. In 1997 she had an annual income of Rs. 7,000 in 1996. In 1997 she cultivated ginger and turmeric in 30 cents of lands under economic self-reliance prorgamme and and earns a profit of Rs. 6,000.

Case Study 2

Pragati and Gramin Bank have persuaded and interacted with women of Sindhiput village of Nandapur block to form a WSHG called Champa Golapi Mahi la Sangh with 17 woman members, with monthly saving of Rs. 10 per member. Pragati has provided an amount of Rs. 2,000 to the SHG for taking up income generation activities in goat rearing, leaf plate making and vegetable cultivation. The SHG was prompt in repayment of loans. It has opened a SB account with KPG bank at Padwa. Pragati has taken initiative in imparting training to womean members in leaf plate making and capacity building. Previously they were selling *siali* leaves collected from forest bundles, whereas now they are preparing leaf plates and selling them in the weekly markets. Thanks to the endeavour of Pragati, today the SHG is in possession of an oil expeller unit which it is operating to earn an income of Rs. 100 per month by crushing oil seeds brought by women of the village. The total loan of woman members of the groups is Rs. 7,550 on August 2001. Of late, the District Civil Supplies Department has directed 300 women self- groups to buy paddy directly from villagers and pay immediately as per government support prices. The purchase of paddy from local *mandis* by MSHGs has resulted in curbing distress sales of paddy and keeping middlemen at bay. The SHGs takes money from their own sources, to buy paddy and sell it to District Civil Supplies Department. The department has fixed Rs. 100 as commission for quintal of paddy transitioning Rs. 1 crore (*The New Indian Express* 13, January 2008).

SELF-HELP GROUPS IN ORISSA

The Government of Orissa is committed to provide credit link plan for self-help group in every village, extend quality micro-finance to over 45 Lakh rural women and for poor families by 2008 and provide a minimum loan amount if Rs.40,000 per group (vision Document prepared under Mission Sakti 2007) (*New Indian Express*, October 25). It is apparent from data furnished by State level Banking Committee Sources (SLBC) that, the total amount of credit provided to 84000 SHGk is reckoned at Rs. 284 crore.

Present SHG-Bank Linkage programme (on 30-11-2006) Total SHGs formed in the State (cumulative) : 214463

1. Government Agencies - 1,32,715
2. NCOS - 6,30,42
3. Banks - 15,384
4. By Others - 3,322
5. Total SHGC Credit linked (Cumulative) under SBLP - 1,95,845.
6. Total SHGS report linked (Cumulative) under SBLP - 43,105.
7. Total Loan to SHGC - Rs. 5,5514 crore cumulative.

Source : *Eleventh plan and Annual Plan*; 2007-08, Govrnment of Orissa, Planning and Co-ordination Department.

Socio-economic Characteristics of Koraput District

Koraput district has a congenial atmosphere for growth of self-help groups particularly composing of women, who are not only amenable to discipline and group dynamics but also contribute to family's income by restoring to wage employment, doing petty business, participating agricultural operations. Koraput district is inhabited by 10,29,577 people. The district has a high per centage of depressed population, low literacy level of people (36.20per cent) poor communication, transport facilities and poor rural electrification (66.74per cent).

Koraput district being predominant tribal, acutely poor and highly backward, SHGs assume great importance to further the cause of the poor. As such, while the coordinating efforts shall be continued vigorously in future, there has been further augmentation of policy initiatives to spearhead the programme at a foster pace at under :

- Induction of NGS Partners
- Involving RRB as SHPI
- Involving Individuals in SHG Promotion
- Providing promotional grant for SHG promotion.
- Saving and thrift habits may be promoted among SHGS.

Banks and NGOs may have to supervise the end use of credit provided to SHGs for crop production purpose to as to transform static credit into dynamic credit.

Static credit means there is no surplus in the hands of farmers after loan recovery for fresh investment in land. Credit is deemed dynamic when farmer has surplus at his this disposal after recovery of loans for fresh investment.

Prof. Yunus has observed that credit to mothers and women brings greater benefits to family than men because women have greater vision and are excellent managers of scarce resources. The WSHGs in Bangladesh have enabled women to come out of poverty, improved nutrition, facilitated in better sanitation, lowered child mortality rate and better access to education.

In the ensuing years, SHGs may widen the range of their vision and perspective to beyond meeting credit needs. Sending children to stay in schools, committing to build a good house for oneself, keeping families small, taking joint decisions to help community, not accepting or giving dowry, drinking clean water, growing vegetables and keeping environment clean. Poverty is not created by the poor but institutions and policies which surround them. So, appropriate changes maybe made in the institutions to contain poverty.

REFERENCES

Basic Potential linked credit plan for X Plan period Koraput NARBARD.

Eleventh Plan and Annual Plan 2007-2008, Government of Orissa.

"Micro Credit & Self-help Groups in Orissa" Dr. B. Eswar Rao Pattnaik & Simanchal Mishra, paper presented at Orissa Economic Conference Bhadrak College, Bhadrak.

New Indian Express, Bhubaneswar.

Prof. Mohammad Younus "Grameen Banks Micro credit & Millenium Development Goals" *Economic & Political Weekly, Sept.* 4-10, 2004 XXXIV (36).

Rudar Dutt and K.P.M. Sundaram, *Indian Economic*.